Psychology Research Progress

COGNITIVE-BEHAVIORAL AND NEUROPSYCHOLOGICAL MODELS OF OBSESSIVE-COMPULSIVE DISORDER

New Spiritual Consciousness and the Transformation of Personality
Ferenc Margitics (Author)
2010. 978-1-61668-253-8

Police Psychology
James M. Peters (Editor)
2010. 978-1-60876-996-4

Environmental Psychology: New Developments
Jorge Valentín and Lucila Gamez (Editors)
2010. 978-1-60876-911-7

Cognitive Psychology Perspectives
Giacomo Salvati and Valeria Rabuano (Editors)
2010. 978-1-60876-059-6

Significance of Individual Aspirations in Health Psychology
Margitics Ferenc and Zsuzsa Pauwlik (Authors)
2010. 978-1-60876-124-1

Category-Specificity: Evidence for Modularity of Mind
Keith R. Laws, Rebecca L. Adlington,
F. Javier Moreno-Martinez and Tim M. Gale (Authors)
2010. 978-1-60876-643-7

Cognitive Deficit in Mental and Neurological Disorders
Hana Kucerova and Marek Preiss (Editors)
2010. 978-1-60741-957-0

Developmental Psychology
Johan Håkansson (Editor)
2010. 978-1-61668-342-9

Stress in the Year 2010 and Beyond
Michael F. Shaughnessy (Editor)
2010. 978-1-60876-444-0

PSYCHOLOGY RESEARCH PROGRESS

Psychology Research Yearbook, Volume 1
Alexandra M. Columbus (Editor)
2009. 978-1-60741-573-2

Jung Today: Volume 1- Adulthood
Francesco Bisagni , Nadia Fina
and Caterina Vezzoli (Editors)
2009. 978-1-60741-893-1

Suicide and the Creative Arts
Steven Stack and David Lester (Editors)
2009. 978-1-60741-958-7

Psychological Scientific Perspectives on
Out of Body and Near Death Experiences
Craig D. Murray (Editor)
2009. 978-1-60741-705-7

Jung Today: Volume 2- Childhood and Adolescence
Francesco Bisagni, Nadia Fina and Caterina Vezzoli (Editors)
2009. 978-1-60741-894-8

Psychology of Burnout: Predictors and Coping Mechanisms
Rachel V. Schwartzhoffer (Editor)
2009. 978-1-60876-010-7

Perchance to Dream: The Frontiers of Dream Psychology
Stanley Krippner and Debbie Joffe Ellis (Authors)
2009. 978-1-60876-123-4

Neuropsychology of the Sense of Agency
Michela Balconi (Author)
2010. 978-1-60876-358-0

The Psychological Impact of Living Under Violence and Poverty in Brazil
Giovanni Marcos Lovisi, Jair de Jesus Mari and Elie S. Valencia (Editors)
2010. 978-1-60876-587-4

What Philosophers Say Compared with What Psychologists Find in Discerning Values: How Wise People Interpret Life
Dolores Pushkar, Sheila Mason, Andrew Burr, Sarah Etezadi and Tracy Lyster (Authors)
2010. 978-1-60876-660-4

Sustainable Evidence-Based Decision-Making
Francesco Chiappelli (Author)
2010. 978-1-60876-665-9

Children's Dreams
Barbara Szmigielska (Author)
2010. 978-1-60876-704-5

A Multiple Self Theory of Personality
David Lester (Author)
2010. 978-1-60876-783-0

Addiction to Exercise: A Symptom or a Disorder?
Attila Szabo (Author)
2010. 978-1-60876-789-2

Community Psychology: New Developments
Niklas Lange and Marie Wagner (Editors)
2010. 978-1-60876-858-5

Regulatory Fit and Persuasion Through Advocacy Messages and Narratives
Leigh Ann Vaughn (Author)
2010. 978-1-60876-887-5

Psychopathology in Juvenile Delinquents
Katerina Maniadaki, Efthymios Kakouros and Rania Karaba (Authors)
2010. 978-1-60876-975-9

Traffic Psychology: An International Perspective
Dwight Hennessy (Editor)
2010. 978-1-61668-846-2

Neuroticism: The Personality Risk Factor for Stress and Impaired Health and Well-Being
Sharon Grant (Author)
2010. 978-1-61668-689-5

Cognitive-Behavioral and Neuropsychological Models of Obsessive-Compulsive Disorder
Claudio Sica, Luigi Rocco Chiri, Dean McKay and Marta Ghisi (Authors)
2010. 978-1-61668-841-7

Consciousness, Attention and Meaning
Giorgio Marchetti (Author)
2010. 978-1-61668-960-5

Psychology Research Progress

COGNITIVE-BEHAVIORAL AND NEUROPSYCHOLOGICAL MODELS OF OBSESSIVE-COMPULSIVE DISORDER

CLAUDIO SICA
DEAN MCKAY
LUIGI ROCCO CHIRI
AND
MARTA GHISI

Nova Biomedical
Nova Science Publishers, Inc.
New York

For permission to use material from this book please contact us:
Telephone 631-231-7269; Fax 631-231-8175
Web Site: http://www.novapublishers.com

Library of Congress Cataloging-in-Publication Data

Cognitive-behavioral and neuropsychological models of obsessive-compulsive disorder / Claudio Sica ... [et al.].
p. ; cm.
Includes bibliographical references and index.
ISBN 978-1-61668-841-7 (softcover)
1. Obsessive-compulsive disorder. 2. Cognition disorders. I. Sica, Claudio.
[DNLM: 1. Obsessive-Compulsive Disorder--psychology. 2. Cognition. WM 176 C676 2010]
RC533.C634 2010
616.85'227--dc22 2010015598

Published by Nova Science Publishers, Inc. † New York

CONTENTS

PREFACE

Obsessive compulsive disorder (OCD) is characterized by persistent, intrusive, and distressing obsessions (unwanted thoughts, impulses, or images) that may or may not be accompanied by compulsions (repetitive behaviors or mental acts). It is a severe and persistent psychological problem with significant negative effects on the individuals' social, family, and occupational functioning.

The book reports on recent research examining phenomenology (included the current debate about its categorization in forthcoming DSM-V), neurobiology (including neuropsychological test data and functional neuroimaging studies), psychological models (including the promising role of so-called "Not Just Right Experiences"), and computational modeling (i.e., neural network) of obsessive-compulsive disorder.

For each of these branch of research, specific limitations in depicting the full scope of OCD will be highlighted. Suggestion on how to go further in order to improve our comprehension of this disorder are also provided.

This book is designed to offer a general view of the state-of-the art of the most recent psychological and neurobiological research on OCD to researchers, psychologists, psychiatrists, mental-health professionals and students.

It reveals essential for a thorough and up to date knowledge and comprehension of this debilitating disorder, both for research and clinical practice.

Chapter 1

OVERVIEW OF OCD

ABSTRACT

Obsessive compulsive disorder (OCD) is characterized by persistent, intrusive, and distressing obsessions (unwanted thoughts, impulses, or images) that may or may not be accompanied by compulsions (repetitive behaviors or mental acts). It is a severe and persistent psychological problem with significant negative effects on the individuals' social, family, and occupational functioning. In this chapter we described the main characteristics of this disorder and its genetic and psychological components, providing also up-to-date epidemiological data. We then reported about the current debate regarding the diagnostic status of OCD: many authors consider OCD as a part of a larger spectrum condition including body dysmorphic disorder, hypochondriasis, Tourette syndrome and trichotillomania, rather than an anxiety disorder. Lastly, the main treatment approaches for OCD as well as their efficacy were described.

INTRODUCTION

Obsessive-compulsive disorder (OCD) is a debilitating syndrome characterized by the presence of obsessions and compulsions. Obsessions are persistent, intrusive, and distressing images, thoughts, or impulses; compulsions are repetitive behaviors or mental acts that these patients feel driven to perform to prevent or reduce distress or to prevent some feared event or situation. Despite the patients recognition that the obsessions and compulsions are unreasonable and the products of their own mind, such phenomenon cause marked distress because they are a source of significant anxiety and interfere with many aspects of social and occupational functioning (Leon, Portera & Weissman, 1995; Koran, Thienemann & Davenport, 1996).

Although OCD is composed of multiple clinical presentations associated with many different types of obsessional concerns and compulsive behaviors, the Diagnostic and Statistical Manual of Mental Disorders (DSM-IV; American Psychiatric Association [APA], 2000) offers a general definition of OCD that includes obsessions and/or compulsions (either may be present in conjunction with or in the absence of the other).

OCD represents one of the most incapacitating of the anxiety disorders owing to its intensity, the continuous and unchanging or deteriorative course of its symptoms and the impairments in interpersonal and occupational functioning that it causes (Rasmussen and Tsuang, 1986; Koran, Thienemann & Davenport, 1996; Antony, Downie & Swinson, 1998; Skoog & Skoog, 1999). The World Health Organization (1996) rated OCD the world's fourth most common mental disorder and one of the top 10 causes worldwide of 'years lived with illness-related disability' (Murray & Lopez, 1996). The burden of OCD at a population level is considerable; e.g., a study in the US estimated the economic cost of OCD to be $8.4 billion in 1990 (DuPont, Rice, Shiraky & Rowland, 1995).

1.1. Epidemiological Data

The lifetime prevalence rate of OCD has been consistently estimated at 2–3% in the general adult population (Angst, 1994; Karno, Golding, Sorenson & Burnam, 1988; Weissman et al., 1994; Rasmussen & Eisen, 1992; Bebbington, 1998; Sasson et al., 1997). Moreover, the data suggested considerable cross-cultural homogeneity in patients, cultural differences being mostly related to the content and frequency of obsessions (Attiullah, Eisen & Rasmussen, 2000; Fontenelle, Mendlowicz, Marques & Versiani, 2004; Sica, Novara, Sanavio, Coradeschi, & Dorz, 2002; Sica, Taylor, Arrindell & Sanavio, 2006). As regards the issue of race in OCD there is still controversy regarding the role of such dimension as a predisposition factor for the development of disorder, and more studies seem appropriate to better understand the contribution of race on OCD (Fontenelle & Hasler, 2008).

The data from epidemiological and clinical studies suggest that OCD typically begins during late adolescence or early adulthood (Myers, Weissman, Tischler et al, 1984; Rasmussen & Tsuang, 1986; Weissman et al., 1994). In clinical samples, the male: female ratio is usually around unity (Rasmussen and Eisen, 1992), while in epidemiological samples, females tend to be slightly more commonly represented than males (Karno et al., 1988; Weissman et al., 1994; Bebbington, 1998). This discrepancy between clinical and epidemiological samples may reflect a difference between men and women in help-seeking behavior, in the degree to which OCD can be tolerated and accommodated by family members, and in occupational expectations (Castle & Groves, 2000). Phenomenological differences seem to exist between men and women with OCD. More men have obsessions with sexual, exactness, or symmetry content; women are more likely to have aggressive obsessions and cleaning rituals (Lensi, Cassano, Correddu, Ravagli & Kunovac 1996). Also, other studies have reported that women are more likely to engage in washing and cleaning compulsions (Castle, Deale & Marks, 1995; Drummond, 1993; Noshirvani, Kasvikis, Marks, Tsakiris & Monteiro 1991).

The average age at first onset of OCD is consistently estimated to be 19–21 years (Flament et al., 1988; Rasmussen and Eisen, 1990). However, this average age of onset is marked by significant variance. In a clinical sample, men had a significantly earlier onset of illness (mean age of onset, 19.5 for men versus 22.0 for women; $p < 0.003$) (Rasmussen & Eisen, 1990). Prepubertal onset of OCD is not rare. In fact, Rapoport (1990) indicated that 30% to 50% of adults with OCD report childhood onset and as many as one third of OCD patients recall symptoms emerging before the age of 15 years. Similarly, Rasmussen and Eisen (1990) showed that the onset was before age 14 for 21% of 830 patients and before age 12 for 11% of patients. Moreover, in adults, there is some epidemiological evidence suggesting that aging leads to a reduction in the prevalence rates of obsessive–compulsive symptoms (Degonda et al., 2003) and clinically recognized OCD (Fireman, Koran, Leventhal & Jacobson, 2001). Çilli et al. (2004) substained that this may be particularly true for males: they found that the 1-year prevalence of adult OCD was inversely related to age in males, while it increased with age in females. In the study by Crino, Slade & Andrews (2005), older individuals (N > 55 years) were significantly less likely than those in younger age groups to have OCD. In short, these findings suggest that older adolescents may be particularly prone to develop OCD, while older individuals may display OCD less frequently.

OCD is much more likely to develop in boys than girls before age 10 years (Leonard et al., 1993); male predominance has been observed in 67% of 70 OCD subjects between ages of 6 and 18 years (Leonard et al., 1989). Therefore, it seems that males develop OCD at a younger age than do females

(Attiullah et al., 2000) and the greater frequency of later onset OCD in women may be partially explained by the association of depression and OCD (Noshirvani et al., 1991). However, this issue is far from being settled. For example, in studies that employed the Leyton Obsessional Inventory—Children's Version as a screening instrument in samples of children and adolescents, females reported significantly more symptoms and interference than boys in almost all items (Flament et al., 1988; Thomsen & Mikkelsen, 1993; King, Ollendick & Montgomery, 1995; Maggini et al., 2001; Brynska & Wolanczyk, 2005). It is conceivable, therefore, that while girls exhibit more obsessive–compulsive symptoms, boys present more full-blown, severe, and/or impairment generating OCD.

With regard to the marital status, patients being treated for OCD in several countries are less likely to be married than their non-afflicted counterparts (Fontenelle et al., 2004), and similar results have been found some epidemiological samples (Karno et al., 1988; Crum & Anthony, 1993; Grabe et al., 2000; Mohammadi et al., 2004; Çilli et al., 2004; Crino et al., 2005). OCD was more prevalent among divorced or separated subjects than among those who were married or single (Karno et al., 1988). Other studies were unable to find differences in the marital status of patients with and without OCD (Mohammadi et al.,2004; Crino et al., 2005) and obsessive–compulsive symptoms (Degonda et al., 2003) or reported results in tight contradiction with the above mentioned ones (Nestadt et al., 1994). Probably, for each psychiatric disorder examined, marital status (divorce or separated) was also a significant correlate, suggesting that this status was not specific for OCD (Fontenelle & Hasler, 2008). Similarly, in a Turkish study, Çilli et al. (2004) reported that the divorced, separated, or widowed subjects had approximately 4.2 times the probability of exhibiting OCD.

1.2. Clinical and Psychiatric Evidence

OCD is associated with high degrees of psychiatric comorbidity. Major depression is the disorder most commonly found associated with OCD with a lifetime rate of 67% (Rasmussen & Eisen, 1992). Other psychiatric conditions seen relatively frequently with OCD are simple phobia (22%), social phobia (18%), eating disorders (17%), alcohol abuse or dependence (14%), panic disorder (12%) and Tourette syndrome (7%) (Rasmussen & Eisen, 1992). Moreover, Attiullah et al. (2000) observed substantial phenomenological overlap between tic disorders and OCD; in fact, certain OCD symptoms, such as symmetry and ordering, are more common among patients with OCD and tic disorders compared with OCD alone.

Increased comorbidity of depression (Noshirvani et al., 1991; Castle et al., 1995), eating disorders (Bogetto, Venturello, Albert, Maina & Ravizza 1999; Castle et al., 1995; Lennkh et al., 1998; Noshirvani et al., 1991) and panic disorder (Lensi et al., 1996) has been reported in females with OCD. In contrast, increased comorbidity of social phobia (Bogetto et al., 1999; Marks, 1987), substance-related disorders (Bogetto et al., 1999; Noshirvani et al., 1991), and hypomanic episodes (Bogetto et al., 1999; Lensi et al., 1996) has been noted in males with OCD. Finally, the heterogeneity and complexity of OCD extends to eating disorders. Rothenberg (1986) found a significant association between a range of obsessive-compulsive characteristics and the presence of an eating disorder. These characteristics were: excessive cleanliness, excessive orderliness, perfectionism, rigidity, fear of change, miserliness, scrupulousness, and self-righteousness.

A few studies have analyzed the patterns of comorbidities in epidemiological sample of childhood OCD (Flament et al., 1988; Zohar et al., 1992, Douglass et al., 1995; Heyman et al., 2001; Peterson et al., 2001; Guerrero et al., 2003). The first was a high school-based study performed by Flament et al. (1988), who found that 75% of children and adolescents with OCD had one or more lifetime psychiatric diagnoses and 50% had at least one other current diagnosis, including major depression (25%), overanxious disorder (20%), compulsive personality disorder (17%), and bulimia nervosa (17%). In a prospective study, Douglass et al. (1995) found that only depression and substance use in early adolescence were risk factors for OCD in young adulthood.

As previously mentioned, experts have recognized that the manifestations of the condition may be marked by a heterogeneous set of dimensions in adults (McKay, et al., 2004) and children (Mataix-Cols, et al., 2008; McKay et al., 2006). Much of the accumulated research examining dimensions has arisen from factor analytic studies of the Yale-Brown Obsessive-Compulsive Scale (YBOCS; Goodman et al., 1989a,b) symptom checklist. The dimensions observed most consistently fall into four broad categories: (1) obsessions (including aggressive, sexual, religious and somatic) and checking compulsions, (2) symmetry and ordering obsessions, and counting compulsions, (3) contamination obsessions and cleaning compulsions, and (4) hoarding (Abramowitz, McKay, & Taylor, 2005; see also Baer, 1994; Leckman, Grice, Boardman, 1997; Mataix-Cols et al., 1999; Summerfeldt, Richter, Antony & Swinson, 1999). The most frequent types of obsessions are contamination (45%), pathological doubt (42%), somatic (36%), need for symmetry (31%), aggressive (28%), sexual (26%) and other (13%). The classical forms of compulsions include checking (63%), washing (50%), counting (36%), the need to ask or confess (31%), symmetry and precision (28%) and hoarding (18%) (Rasmussen & Eisen, 1992; Sasson et al., 1997). Patients with OCD may report only one (Stein, Forde, Anderson & Walker, 1997) or, more typically, multiple symptoms (Antony et al., 1998). It is important to stress that recent research raises questions about whether hoarding symptoms represent a "pure" dimension of OCD or a separate type of mental health problem (Grisham, Brown, Liverant & Campbell-Sills, 2005; Petusa et al., 2008; Wu & Watson, 2003). For instance, Grisham and colleagues (2005) found evidence that in absence of other obsessions and compulsions, hoarding is likely distinct from OCD.

Approximately 25% of OCD patients report distressing obsessions without overt compulsive rituals. In such clinical presentation, common obsessional themes are sex, harm/violence, and religion/blasphemy. Patients characterized by these symptoms often appraise their distressing thoughts as dangerous, overly important, and hence they try to control such thoughts (Obsessive Compulsive Cognitions Working Group [OCCWG], 2001). Specifically, mental rituals and neutralizing (e.g., reciting ''good'' words after having a ''bad'' thought, counting, and praying) may be carried out to decrease anxiety associated with intrusions.

1.3. Genetic and Psychological Components

It is hard to establish the potential genetic components of pathophysiology of OCD because the investigations are still scarce and the family and twin studies provide mixed conclusions.

A large number of association studies assessing likely candidate genes have now been conducted (Hemmings & Stein, 2006; for a recent review). Generally, association studies have focused on genes that are important to the serotonin and dopaminergic neurotransmitter systems, while some have pursued genes associated with Central Nervous System developmental pathways.

Some data has shown a significant association between OCD in the probands and OCD in their first-degree relatives (Hettema, Neale & Kendler, 2001; Pauls, Alsobrook, Goodman, Rasmussen & Leckman, 1995; Nestadt et al., 2000; see also, Chamberlain et al., 2008; Rector, Cassin, Richter &

Burroughs, 2009). Moreover, a family history of OCD seems to be relatively common, occurring in approximately 25–30% of children and adolescents with severe primary OCD (Swedo, Rapoport, Leonard, Lenane & Cheslow, 1989; Lenane et al., 1990). In a recent family study of nontreatment seeking individuals, the prevalence of OCD among first-degree relatives of affected individuals was 10.3% and that among first-degree relatives of controls was 1.2% (Grabe et al., 2006). These finding clearly support and validate the findings on familiality of OCD in clinical samples, and are of special interest because of the absence of selection bias that might occur as a result of treatment seeking behavior for OCD or comorbid disorders that could have triggered treatment seeking (Grabe et al., 2006). Finally, all but one study (Fyer et al., 2005) that have investigated the familiarity of OCD according to the age of onset in probands found that family history may be particularly related to early-onset (Nestadt et al., 2000; Reddy et al., 2001; do Rosario-Campos et al., 2005; Hanna et al., 2005).

Twin and adoption studies may help to shed light on the roles played by genes in the etiology of OCD. While adoption studies are generally rare and are not available in the OCD literature, at least 28 twin studies of patients with obsessive–compulsive symptoms have been published with different methodologies and mixed results (as reviewed by van Grootheest et al., 2005). van Grootheest et al. (2005) argued that only studies using Structural Equation Modeling have convincingly shown that obsessive–compulsive symptoms are heritable, with genetic influences in the range of 45% to 65% in children and 27% to 47% in adults.

Also, different symptom clusters and dimensions have been related to different patterns of genetic transmission (Alsobrook, Leckman, Goodman, Rasmussen & Pauls, 1999; Tourette Syndrome Association International Consortium for Genetics [TSAICG], 2003), comorbidity (Baer, 1994; Mataix-Cols et al., 1999; Mataix-Cols, Baer, Rauch & Jenike, 2000; Samuels et al., 2002) and treatment response (Mataix-Cols et al., 1999; Mataix-Cols, Marks, Greist, Kobak & Baer 2002; Black et al., 1998; Saxena et al., 2002).

The broad range of symptoms seen in OCD along with the differential response to treatment has caused some difficulty in etiological definition and clinical intervention with such disorder. Among etiological theories, cognitive-behavioral models of OCD have generated a large body of empirical support and have led to the development of effective treatments (Frost & Steketee, 2002). These models suggest that dysfunctional beliefs and maladaptive appraisals underlie unhelpful strategies in the management of intrusive phenomena. Such strategies lead to drastic reactions to specific intrusive thoughts, images, or urges resulting in obsessive and compulsive symptoms (Clark & Purdon, 1993; de Silva & Rachman, 1998; Rachman, 1998; Salkovskis, 1985). Obsessive Compulsive Cognitions Working Group (OCCWG, 1997) has highlighted six main belief domains that play an important role in the development of obsessions from intrusive thoughts: over-importance of thought, inflated personal responsibility, overestimation of threat, intolerance for uncertainty, beliefs about the importance of controlling one's thoughts, and perfectionism. Recently, the OCCWG (Steketee et al., 2003; Taylor, Kyrios, Thordarson, Steketee, & Frost, 2002) reported not only a high degree of association between the identified belief domains and OC symptoms, but also high intercorrelations between scales measuring the six domains. This raises questions about possible higher order cognitive vulnerabilities that may account for such high intercorrelations.

Similar to other anxiety disorders (Bolton et al., 2006), the etiology of OCD is likely to involve both environmental and genetic factors and interactions between them. For this reason, gene by environment (G $^{\times}$ E) studies of OCD are essential (Grisham, Anderson & Sachdev, 2008).

1.4. The DSM-V Debate

A current debate concerns the exact nature of OCD and its reclassification into a larger spectrum of disorders for the forthcoming Diagnostic and Statistical Manual—Fifth Edition.

For some researchers a reason to move away OCD from anxiety disorders category is that anxiety is a relatively non-specific symptom associated with a number of other psychiatric disorders (e.g., depression, bipolar disorder, and schizophrenia). Thus, although conceptualizing OCD as an anxiety disorder may be useful from a diagnostic perspective, ultimately it does little to further the understanding of OCD and to address questions related to the etiology and treatment of this disorder (Bartz & Hollander, 2006).

Other clinicians and researchers disagree with such position. In Mataix-Cols et al. (2007) survey, 40% of 187 mental health professionals who specialized in OCD treatment and research considered OCD as an anxiety disorder and disagreed with a category shift. The main reasons for disagreeing were that OCD and other anxiety disorders respond to similar treatments and tend to co-occur.

1.4.1. OCD as Spectrum Disorder

Over the past decade, a wide variety of psychiatric and medical conditions has progressively motivated to consider OCD spectrum disorders. Body dysmorphic disorder (BDD) and hypochondriasis (among somatoform disorders), Tourette syndrome (among tic disorders) and trichotillomania, pathological gambling or kleptomania (among impulse control disorders) have been shown to share apparent similarities with OCD regarding clinical symptomatology, demographic, comorbidity and family history characteristics, course pattern, heritability, brain circuitry, neurotransmitter abnormalities and responses to pharmacological and psychological therapeutic strategies (for review, see McElroy, Phillips & Keck, 1994; Hollander et al., 2007; Hollander & Wong, 1995).

The impulse-control disorders are thought to belong to the OCD spectrum on the basis of the dimensional concept of compulsivity/risk-aversion versus impulsivity/novelty seeking (McElroy et al., 1994; Hollander and Wong, 1995; Stein, 2000). In this perspective, compulsivity may be considered as associated with harm avoidance, whereas impulsivity appears more harmful, less senseless, more spontaneous and leading to pleasure and gratification. Therefore, OCD falls at the compulsive end of the OCD spectrum, whereas impulsive disorders lie more toward the impulsivity end. Moreover, some authors affirmed that anorexia nervosa and bulimia nervosa may belong to the family of obsessive-compulsive spectrum disorders (McElroy et al., 1994).

But, which are the evidences supporting OCD as spectrum disorder? For instance, Richter et al. (2003) found that compared to a panic disorder and social phobia groups, OCD group had a greater number of individuals suffering from any (clinical or subclinical) lifetime spectrum disorder, and individuals in the OCD group were affected by a greater number of spectrum conditions. In examining data from a large family study, Bienvenu et al. (2000) found that case probands (with OCD) had elevated prevalence rates of body dysmorphic disorder, hypochondriasis, anorexia and bulimia nervosa, and grooming disorders. With respect to first-degree relatives, elevated prevalence rates were found for hypochondriasis, body dysmorphic disorder, and all grooming disorders compared to relatives of control probands. Also, the lifetime prevalence of Tourette's syndrome and tic disorders (e.g., transient tic disorder, and chronic motor and vocal tics) has been found to be greater in relatives of OCD patients compared to relatives of controls (Grados et al., 2001).

Other authors considered the differences between OCD and anxiety disorders. Research on pathophysiology of OCD suggests an involvement of frontal–striatal circuitry, whereas pathophysiological models of anxiety disorders point to the amygdala and associated fear neurocircuitry (see next chapters). OCD is associated with dysregulation of the dopaminergic and serotonergic systems. With the exception of social anxiety disorder, there is little evidence of dopamine dysregulation in other anxiety disorders. Lastly, many anxiety disorders- but not OCD - are characterized by GABA dysregulation. In fact, anxiety disorders except OCD respond to benzodiazepines, which are GABA agonists (Bartz & Hollander, 2006)

1.4.2. OCD as Anxiety Disorder

While there have been forceful arguments in favour of a spectrum of obsessive-compulsive disorders, others have countered that the evidence does not support such a wide range of conditions falling under the umbrella of the spectrum (McKay, Abramowitz,, & Taylor, 2008). For example, whereas proponents of the spectrum cite overlap between impulsive symptoms across candidate spectrum disorders, closer examination of the data show the overlap is primarily among disorders of similar kind (i.e., candidate impulsive based disorders correlate highly with impulsive symptoms; candidate compulsive disorders correlate with compulsive symptoms).

Storch, Abramowitz and Goodman (2008) provided a critical analysis of claims in favor of OCD as spectrum disorder. First of all, these authors argued that "repetitive behaviors" is a too vague criteria for identifying a broad category of disorders including OCD, gambling, ''obsessive'' jealousy, etc. As far as OCD is concerned, repetition is simply one of the several means by which patients with OCD neutralize obsessional distress, whereas ''compulsivity'' is simply a way of describing this behavior. Second, what exactly is meant by ''compulsivity,'' ''impulsivity,'' and ''spectrum'' has not been well defined yet. For instance, compulsive behavior in OCD is usually conceptualized as an escape behavior whereas impulsive behavior, such as pathological gambling or kleptomania, is considered pleasure-seeking. It is unclear what kind of data would demonstrate whether these two classes of behavior exist on a spectrum. Third, cognitive-behavioral models of OCD symptoms highlight the role of dysfunctional beliefs and interpretations of situations and normally occurring intrusive thoughts in explaining the persistence of obsessions and compulsions (Rachman, 1998; Salkovskis,

1985), whereas our knowledge of cognitive mechanisms in disorders such as pathological gambling or body dysmorphic disorder is poorer and by far less coherent than in OCD. Fourth, biological studies are still at their infancy and it is premature to support a spectrum disorder through the (inconsistent) evidences driven from these study. Fifth, comorbidity rates between OCD and other anxiety and mood disorders are higher than the rates for any other disorder, including those belonging to a putative spectrum. Lastly, there are insufficient data to support a spectrum disorder as a function of treatment response; on the contrary, Cognitive-Behavior Therapy, onc of the most effective treatment for OCD, is quite similar to that used for other anxiety disorders (e.g.,social phobia and PTSD).

In sum, following Storch et al. (2008), OCD would be better conceptualized as a problem in which an individual is fearful of certain situations and stimuli, which are the focus of the obsessions. Compulsive behavior is then performed with the purpose of alleviating obsessional distress, a phenomenon that unifies OCD with other anxiety disorders. OCD, specific and social phobia, panic, PTSD, and generalized anxiety disorder all involve fear that occurs in the context of more or less disorder-specific situations or stimuli. Research also demonstrates that, across disorders, this fear is maintained by distorted perceptions regarding the dangerousness of such situations, sensations, or mental events (e.g, Barlow, 2002). Lastly, patients with different anxiety disorders respond in a similar way (i.e. avoidance, safety-seeking behaviors, escape) when confronted with feared stimuli.

1.4.3. Current Tendencies

A balanced position is that OCD does not appear to fit well with either the anxiety disorders or any broad spectrum. Symptoms of OCD may be motivated by factors other than fear such as disgust (Stein et al., 2001) and feelings of incompleteness; moreover, a considerable literature has debated the inclusion of hoarding as an OCD subtype (e.g., Grisham et al., 2005), given the often ego-syntonic nature of hoarding symptoms among other characteristics that distinguish it from more ''classic'' OCD symptoms (Lochner et al., 2005). On the other side, it would appear premature to identify a spectrum of obsessive-compulsive disorders since there is still no clear model that adequately describes OCD proper (Taylor, McKay, & Abramowitz, 2005) let alone the complex array of conditions that form the basis of the spectrum.

As proposed by Storch and colleagues (2008), due to the extreme heterogeneity of OCD, it is entirely possible that some OCD symptoms (e.g., contamination) share many features with anxiety disorders, whereas other ones involving symmetry, ordering, and the like may share features with other disorders. In other words, studying and treating OCD as if it was a homogeneous entity seems no longer justified by actual evidences.

In any case, as critiques have accumulated, some prominent advocates of the spectrum have scaled back their claims, and have since substantially narrowed the range of candidate spectrum disorders, and renamed the spectrum "obsessive compulsive related disorders" (Hollander et al., 2008). For instance, from the survey of Mataix-Cols and colleagues (2007) emerged that if a new OCD spectrum disorders category is created, the expert consensus is to keep it narrow and only include body dysmorphic disorder (72% agree), trichotillomania (70% agree), and possibly tic disorders (61% agree) and hypochondriasis (57% agree). A majority of experts disagreed with the inclusion of other disorders classified elsewhere in DSM-IV-TR.

1.5. Treatment Approaches

Longitudinal research on the nature of OCD suggests it is chronic in nature, and does not spontaneously remit (Abramowitz, Taylor, & McKay, in press). Further, aside from schizophrenia, it has the lowest placebo response in pharmacological trials. As far as treatment is concerned, distinct therapeutic approaches have been developed ranging from psychotropic drugs to psychosurgery, including cognitive–behavioral therapies (CBT), and are now considered as effective for the management of OCD. An ample body of literature has emerged and proven the efficacy of antidepressant agents SRIs for treating OCD. Therefore, 5HT-reuptake inhibitor antidepressants may be considered as the first-line treatment of OCD. However, 40–60% of patients with OCD fail to respond adequately, with minimal to no change during treatment with SRIs alone (for review, see Goodman, McDougle & Price, 1992; Goodman, 1999). In these cases of partial or no response, different pharmacological strategies have been proposed, including combinations of SRIs with dopamine receptor antagonists. Adjunction of the prototypical neuroleptic haloperidol proved significantly better than placebo in reducing OCD symptom severity (McDougle, Goodman & Price, 1994).

Psychological treatments primarily based on CBT have demonstrated efficacy in the treatment of OCD, alone or in combination with pharmacotherapy using SRIs. The goal of this treatment is to learn to respond appropriately to intrusive thoughts and urges of OCD in new and much more adaptive ways. The current procedures are in vivo (real-life) exposure with self-imposed response prevention (ERP) and restructuring of the beliefs about intrusive thoughts. ERP and cognitive restructuring (CR) seemed to show a similar effectiveness and theirs combination did not improve the benefits achieved by these two techniques separately (Rosa-Alcazar et al., 2008). Therefore, both ERP and CR proved to be effective treatments to reduce obsessive–compulsive symptoms in patients with OCD. In spite of the lack of studies that offer more clarifying data, and although a clear superiority of ERP over CR has not been proven in terms of effectiveness, Rosa-Alcazar et al. (2008) suggested that the higher simplicity of ERP in comparison with CR constitutes an important advantage for its implementation in professional practice. This, the ERP would be the treatment of choice and more research is required to examine the benefits of CR alone. Recently, Grisham & Williams (2009) proposed that the OCD treatments should promote more adaptive ways of responding to intrusive thoughts. One promising clinical strategy is an acceptance-based approach, which focuses on increasing one's willingness to experience uncomfortable thoughts and feelings without avoiding, struggling with or viewing them as being true (Hayes, Strosahl, & Wilson, 1999). Hayes et al. (1999, 1996) suggested that acceptance is achieved through the absence of control attempts and other forms of experiential avoidance (such as rumination). Indeed, Marcks and Woods (2005) found that nonclinical participants using an acceptance-based strategy experienced a decrease in discomfort level associated with intrusive thoughts (although not thought frequency) compared to suppression. In addition, a recent study has found that acceptance and commitment therapy (ACT) for clinical OCD patients led to a decrease in self-reported compulsions (Twohig, Hayes, & Masuda, 2006). The current findings are also consistent with traditional cognitive-behavioral approaches, particularly exposure and response prevention (ERP), which has demonstrated efficacy in the treatment of OCD (see Abramowitz, 1996). Similar to ACT, ERP techniques address maladaptive response-focused regulation strategies by encouraging patients to experience and tolerate unwanted thoughts and sensations rather than avoid them. Regardless, both treatments may function to reduce the use of thought suppression in response to intrusive thoughts.

Neurosurgical treatments have been considered for the management of chronic, severely distressing forms of OCD resistant to all available conventional treatments. The most frequently described procedures, which are anterior capsulotomy, anterior cingulotomy, subcaudate tractotomy and capsulotomy, have shown to be of significant benefit in the treatment of refractory OCD. (Aouizerate et al., 2004).

Conclusion

The underlying pathophysiology of OCD is still not fully understood. Researchers advocating a pharmacological approach to treatment have recently focused on the possibility of a fear network for the disorder (discussed in Abramowitz, Taylor, & McKay, in press). In fact, a central feature of obsessions and associated compulsions is the presence of doubting. That is, sufferers struggle to determine whether the compulsions have been adequate in alleviating the risk associated with the obsessional idea. This cognitive function, and the ability to form a greater sense of certainty in non-OCD individuals, has been hypothesized to originate in the frontal orbital-striatal area, and the dorsolateral prefrontal cortex. A breakdown in this system is considered the core biological premise underlying OCD. However, as noted in Abramowitz, McKay, and Taylor (in press), a condition with the marked heterogeneity of OCD defies such a clear biological organization.

We are in the need therefore of a better understanding the several etiological factors involved in such condition and to determine the association between specific type of symptoms characteristics and treatment response. Moreover, since almost 80% of all cases beginning during childhood and adolescence (Pauls et al., 1995), pediatric studies could be critical in advancing our understanding of the OCD. Lastly, OCD patients seem vulnerable to a broad spectrum of psychiatric disorders and more studies should actively investigate OCD spectrum disorders, anorexia nervosa, and bipolar disorder as possible predictors of a worse treatment response in OCD (Shavit, Frost, Kushner, Crews & Alexander, 2006).

References

Abramowitz, J. S. (1996). Variants of exposure and response prevention in the treatment of obsessive-compulsive disorder: A meta-analysis. *Behavior Therapy, 27*, 583-600.

Abramowitz, J. S., McKay, D., & Taylor, S. (2005). Introduction to the special section: Subtypes in Obsessive-Compulsive Disorder. *Behavior Therapy, 36*, 367-369.

Abramowitz, J. S., Taylor, S., & McKay, D. (in press). Obsessive-compulsive disorder. *The Lancet.*

Alsobrook, J. P., Leckman, J. F., Goodman, W., Rasmussen, S. A., & Pauls, D. L. (1999). Segregation analysis of obsessive-compulsive disorder using symptom-based factor scores. *American Journal of Medical Genetics, 88*, 669-675.

American Psychiatric Association. (2000). *Diagnostic and statistical manual of mental disorders* (4th ed., text revision). Washington, DC: American Psychiatric Press.

Angst, J. (1994). The epidemiology of obsessive-compulsive disorder. In E. Hollander, J. Zohar, D. Maraziti & B. Oliver (Eds.), *Current insight in obsessive-compulsive disorder* (pp. 93-104). West Sussex, UK: Wiley.

Antony, M. M., Downie, F., & Swinson, R. P. (1998). Diagnostic issues and epidemiology in obsessive-compulsive disorder. In R. P. Antony, S. Rachman & M. A. Richter (Eds.), *Obsessive-compulsive disorder. Theory, research, and treatment* (pp. 3-32). New York: Guilford Press.

Aouizerate, B., Guehl, D., Cuny, E., Rougier, A., Bioulac, B., Tignol, J., et al. (2004). Pathophysiology of obsessive-compulsive disorder: A necessary link between phenomenology, neuropsychology, imagery and physiology. *Progress in Neurobiology, 72*(3), 195-221.

Attiullah, N., Eisen, J. L., & Rasmussen, S. A. (2000). Clinical features of obsessive-compulsive disorder. *Psychiatric Clinics of North America, 23*(3), 469-491.

Baer, L. (1994). Factor analysis of symptom subtypes of obsessive compulsive disorder and their relation to personality and tic disorders. *Journal of Clinical Psychiatry, 55*, 18-23.

Barlow, D. H. (2002). *Anxiety and its disorders: The nature and treatment of anxiety and panic* (2nd ed.). New York, NY, USA: Guilford Press.

Bartz, J. A., & Hollander, E. (2006a). Is obsessive-compulsive disorder an anxiety disorder? *Progress in Neuro-Psychopharmacology & Biological Psychiatry, 30*, 338-352.

Bartz, J. A., & Hollander, E. (2006b). The neuroscience of affiliation: Forging links between basic and clinical research on neuropeptides and social behavior. *Hormones and Behavior, 50*, 518-528.

Bebbington, P. (1998). Epidemiology of obsessive-compulsive disorder. *British Journal of Psychiatry, 173*(suppl 35), 2-6.

Bienvenu, O. J., Samuels, J. F., Riddle, M. A., Hoehn-Saric, R., Liang, K. Y., Cullen, B. A., et al. (2000). The relationship of obsessive–compulsive disorder to possible spectrum disorders: Results from a family study. *Biological Psychiatry, 48*, 287-293.

Black, D. W., Monahan, P., Gable, J., Blum, N., Clany, G., & Baker, P. (1998). Hoarding and treatment response in 38 nondepressed subjects with obsessive-compulsive disorder. *Journal of Clinical Psychiatry, 59*, 420-425.

Bogetto, F., Venturello, S., Albert, U., Maina, G., & Ravizza, L. (1999). Gender-related clinical differences in obsessive-compulsive disorder. *European Psychiatry, 114*, 434-441.

Bolton, D., Eley, T. C., O'Connor, T. G., Perrin, S., Rabe-Hesketh, S., Rijsdijk, F., et al. (2006). Prevalence and genetic and environmental influences on anxiety disorders in 6-year-old twins. *Psychological Medicine, 36*, 335-344.

Brynska, A., & Wolanczyk, T. (2005). Epidemiology and phenomenology of obsessive-compulsive disorder in non-referred young adolescents: A Polish perspective. *European Child & Adolescent Psychiatry, 14*, 319-327.

Castle, D. J., Deale, A., & Marks, I. M. (1995). Gender differences in obsessive compulsive disorder. *Australian and New Zealand Journal of Psychiatry, 29*(114-7).

Castle, D. J., & Groves, A. (2000). The internal and external boundaries of obsessive-compulsive disorder. *Australian and New Zealand Journal of Psychiatry, 34*(2), 249-255.

Chamberlain, S. R., Menzies, L., Hampshire, A., Suckling, J., Fineberg, N. A., del Campo, N., et al. (2008). Orbitofrontal dysfunction in patients with obsessive-compulsive disorder and their unaffected relatives. *Science, 321*(5887), 421-422.

Cilli, A. S., Telcioglu, M., Askin, R., Kaya, N., Bodur, S., & Kucur, R. (2004). Twelve-month prevalence of obsessive-compulsive disorder in Konya, Turkey. *Comprehensive Psychiatry, 45*, 367-374.

Clark, D. A., & Purdon, C. (1993). New perspectives for a cognitive theory of obsessions. *Australian Psychologist, 28*(3), 161-167.

Crino, R., Slade, T., & Andrews, G. (2005). The changing prevalence and severity of obsessive-compulsive disorder criteria from DSM-III to DSM-IV. *The American Journal of Psychiatry, 162*, 876-882.

Crum, R. M., & Anthony, J. C. (1993). Cocaine use and other suspected risk factors for obsessive-compulsive disorder: A prospective study with data from the Epidemiologic Catchment Area surveys. *Drug and Alcohol Dependence, 31*, 281-295.

de Silva, P., & Rachman, S. (1998). *Obsessive-compulsive disorder: The facts* (2nd ed.). New York: Oxford University Press.

Degonda, M., Wyss, M., & Angst, J. (2003). The Zurich Study: XVIII. Obsessive-compulsive disorders and syndromes in the general population. *European Archives of Psychiatry and Clinical Neuroscience, 243*, 16-22.

do Rosario-Campos, M. C., Leckman, J. F., Curi, M., Quatrano, S., Katsovitch, L., Miguel, E. C., et al. (2005). A family study of early-onset obsessive-compulsive disorder. *American Journal of Medeical Genetics. Part B, Neuropsychiatric Genetics 136b*, 92-97.

Douglass, H. M., Moffit, T. E., Dar, R., McGee, R., & Silva, P. (1995). An Epidemiological Study of Obsessive-Compulsive Disorder and Related Disorders in Israeli Adolescents. *Journal of the American Academy of Child & Adolescent Psychiatry, 34*, 1424-1431.

Drummond, L. (1993). The treatment of severe, chronic, resistant obsessive-compulsive disorder: An evaluation of an inpatient programme using behavioral psychotherapy in combination with other treatments. *British Journal of Psychiatry, 163*, 223-229.

DuPont, R. L., Rice, D. P., Shiraki, S., & Rowland, C. R. (1995). Economic costs of obsessive-compulsive disorder. *Medical Interface, 8*, 102-109.

Fireman, B., Koran, L. M., Leventhal, J. L., & Jacobson, A. (2001). The prevalence of clinically recognized obsessive-compulsive disorder in a large health maintenance organization. *The American Journal of Psychiatry, 158*, 1904-1910.

Flament, M. F., Whitaker, A., Rapoport, J. L., Davies, M., Z., B. C., Kalikow, K., et al. (1988). Obsessive compulsive disorder in adolescence: an epidemiological study. *Journal of American Academy of Child and Adolescent Psychiatry, 27*, 764-771.

Fontenelle, L. F., & Hasler, G. (2008). The analytical epidemiology of obsessive-compulsive disorder: Risk factors and correlates. *Progress in Neuro-Psychopharmacology & Biological Psychiatry, 32*, 1-15.

Fontenelle, L. F., Mendlowicz, M. V., Marques, C., & Versiani, M. (2004). Trans-cultural aspects of obsessive-compulsive disorder: A description of a Brazilian sample and a systematic review of international clinical studies. *Journal of Psychiatric Research, 38*, 403-411.

Frost, R. O., & Steketee, G. (2002). *Cognitive approaches to obsessions and compulsions: Theory, assessment, and treatment.* Amsterdam, Netherlands: Pergamon/Elsevier Science Ltd.

Goodman, W. (1999). Obsessive–compulsive disorder: Diagnosis and treatment. *Journal of Clinical Psychiatry, 60*, 27-32.

Goodman, W., McDougle, C. J., & Price, L. H. (1992). Pharmacotherapy of obsessive compulsive disorder. *Journal of Clinical Psychiatry, 53*, 29-37.

Goodman, W. K., Price, L. H., Rasmussen, S. A., Mazure, C., & al, e. (1989a). The Yale-Brown Obsessive Compulsive Scale: I. Development, use, and reliability. *Archives of General Psychiatry, 46*, 1006-1011.

Goodman, W. K., Price, L. H., Rasmussen, S. A., Mazure, C., & al., e. (1989b). The Yale-Brown Obsessive Compulsive Scale: II. Validity. *Archives of General Psychiatry, 46*, 1012-1016.

Grabe, H. J., Meyer, C., Hapke, U., Rumpf, H. J., Freyberger, H. J., Dilling, H., et al. (2000). Prevalence, quality of life and psychosocial function in obsessive-compulsive disorder and subclinical obsessive-compulsive disorder in northern Germany. *European Archives of Psychiatry and Clinical Neuroscience, 250*, 262-268.

Grados, M. A., Riddle, M. A., Samuels, J. F., Liang, K. Y., Hoehn-Saric, R., Bienvenu, O. J., et al. (2001). The familial phenotype of obsessive–compulsive disorder in relation to tic disorders: The Hopkins OCD family study. *Biological Psychiatry, 50*, 559-565.

Grisham, J. R., Anderson, T. M., & Sachdev, P. S. (2008). Genetic and environmental influences on obsessive-compulsive disorder. *European Archives of Psychiatry and Clinical Neuroscience, 258*, 107-116.

Grisham, J. R., Brown, T. A., Liverant, G. I., & Campbell-Sills, L. (2005). The distinctiveness of compulsive hoarding from obsessive-compulsive disorder. *Journal of Anxiety Disorders, 19*(7), 767-779.

Grisham, J. R., & Williams, A. D. (2009). Cognitive control of obsessional thoughts. *Behaviour Research and Therapy, 47*, 395-402.

Guerrero, A. P., Hishinuma, E. S., Andrade, N. N., Bell, C. K., Kurahara, D. K., Lee, T. G., et al. (2003). Demographic and clinical characteristics of adolescents in Hawaii with obsessive-compulsive disorder. *Archives of Pediatrics & Adolescent Medicine, 157*, 665-670.

Hanna, G. L., Fischer, D. J., Chadha, K. R., Himle, J. A., & Van Etten, M. (2005). Familial and Sporadic Subtypes of Early-Onset Obsessive-Compulsive Disorder. *Biological Psychiatry, 57*, 895-900.

Hayes, S. C., Strosahl, K. D., & Wilson, K. G. (Eds.). (1999). *Acceptance and commitment therapy: An experiential approach to behavior change*. New Nork, NY, US: Guilford Press.

Hemmings, S. M. J., & Stein, D. J. (2006). The Current Status of Association Studies in Obsessive-Compulsive Disorder. *Psychiatric Clinics of North America, 29*, 411-444.

Heyman, I., Fombonne, E., Simmons, H., Ford, T., Meltzer, H., & Goodman, R. (2001). Prevalence of obsessive-compulsive disorder in the British nationwide survey of child mental health. *British Journal of Psychiatry, 179*, 324-329.

Hettema, J. M., Neale, M. C., & Kendler, K. S. (2001). A review and meta-analysis of the genetic epidemiology of anxiety disorders. *American Journal of Psychiatry, 158*, 1568-1578.

Hollander, E., Braun, A., & Simeon, D. (2008). Should OCD leave the anxiety disorders in DSM-V? The case for obsessive-compulsive related disorders. *Depression and Anxiety, 25*, 317-329.

Hollander, E., Kim, S., Khanna, S., & Pallanti, S. (2007). Obsessive–compulsive disorder and obsessive–compulsive spectrum disorders: Diagnostic and dimensional issues. *CNS Spectrum, 12*, 5-13.

Hollander, E., & Wong, C. M. (1995). Obsessive–compulsive spectrum disorders. *Journal of Clinical Psychiatry, 56*(suppl 4), 3-6.

Karno, M., Golding, J., Sorenson, S., & Burnam, A. (1988). The epidemiology of obsessive-compulsive disorder in five US communities. *Archives of General Psychiatry, 45*(12), 1094-1099.

King, N. J., Ollendick, T. H., & Montgomery, I. M. (1995). Obsessive-compulsive disorder in children and adolescents. *Behaviour Change, 12*, 51-58.

Koran, L. M., Thienemann, M. L., & Davenport, R. (1996). Quality of life for patients with obsessive-compulsive disorder. *American Journal of Psychiatry, 153*, 783-788.

Leckman, J. F., Grice, D. E., Boardman, J., & Zhang, H. (1997). Simptoms of obsessive-compulsive disorder. *American Journal of Psychiatry, 154*(7), 911-917.

Lenane, M. C., Swedo, S. E., Leonard, H. L., Pauls, D. L., Sceery, W., & Rapoport, J. L. (1990). Psychiatric disorders in first degree relatives of children and adolescents with obsessive compulsive disorder. *Journal of American Academy of Child and Adolescent Psychiatry, 29*, 407-412.

Lennkh, S., Stmad, A., Bailer, D., Fodor, G., & de Zwaan, M. (1998). Comorbidity of obsessive-compulsive disorder in patients with eating disorders. *Eat and Weight Disorders, 3*, 37-41.

Lensi, P., Cassano, G., Correddu, G., Ravagli, S., & Kunovac, J. J. (1996). Obsessive-compulsive disorder. Familial-developmental history, symptomatology, comorbidity and course with special reference to gender-related differences. *British Journal of Psychiatry, 169*(1), 101-107.

Leon, A. C., Portera, L., & Weissman, M. M. (1995). The social costs of anxiety disorders. *British Journal of Psychiatry, 166*(suppl 27), 19-22.

Leonard, H. L., Swedo, S. E., Lenane, M. C., Rettew, D. C., Hamburger, S. D., Bartko, J. J., et al. (1993). A 2- to 7-year follow-up study of 54 obsessive-compulsive children and adolescents. *Archives of General Psychiatry, 50*(6), 429-439.

Leonard, H. L., Swedo, S. E., Rapoport, J. L., Koby, E. V., Lenane, M. C., Cheslow, D. L., et al. (1989). Treatment of obsessive-compulsive disorder with clomipramine and desipramine in children and adolescents. A double-blind crossover comparison. *Archives of General Psychiatry, 46*(12), 1088-1092.

Lochner, C., Kinnear, C. J., Hemmings, S. M., Seller, C., Niehaus, D. J., Knowles, J. A., et al. (2005). Hoarding in obsessive–compulsive disorder: Clinical and genetic correlates. *Journal of Clinical Psychiatry, 66*, 1155-1160.

Maggini, C., Ampollini, P., Gariboldi, S., Cella, P. L., Pellizza, L., & Marchesi, C. (2001). The Parma High School Epidemiological Survey: Obsessive-compulsive symptoms. *Acta Psychiatrica Scandinavica, 103*, 441-446.

Marcks, B. A., & Woods, D. W. (2005). A comparison of thought suppression to an acceptance-based technique in the management of personal intrusive thoughts: A controlled evaluation. *Behaviour Research and Therapy, 43*, 433-445.

Marks, I. M. (1987). *Fears, phobias, and rituals: Panic, anxiety, and their disorders*. New York: Oxford University Press.

Mataix-Cols, D., Baer, L., Rauch, S. L., & Jenike, M. A. (2000). Relation of factor-analyzed dimensions of obsessive-compulsive disorder to personality disorders. *Acta Psychiatrica Scandinavica, 102*, 199-202.

Mataix-Cols, D., Junque, C., Sanchez-Turet, M., Vallejo, J., Verger, K., & Barrios, M. (1999). Neuropsychological functioning in a subclinical obsessive-compulsive sample. *Biological Psychiatry, 45*(7), 898-904.

Mataix-Cols, D., Marks, I. M., Greist, J. H., Kobak, K. A., & Baer, L. (2002). Obsessive-compulsive symptom dimensions as predictors of compliance with and response to behaviour therapy: Results from a controlled trial. *Psychotherapy and Psychosomatics, 71*, 255-262.

Mataix-Cols, D., Nakatani, E., Micali, N., & Heyman, I. (2008). Structure of obsessive-compulsive symptoms in pediatric OCD. *Journal of the American Academy of Child and Adolescent Psychiatry, 47*, 773-778.

Mataix-Cols, D., Pertusa, A., & Leckman, J. F. (2007). Issues for DSM-V: How should obsessive-compulsive and related disorders be classified? *American Journal of Psychiatry, 164*, 1313-1314.

Mataix-Cols, D., Rauch, S. L., Manzo, P. A., Jenike, M. A., & Baer, L. (1999). Use of factor-analyzed symptom dimensions to predict outcome with serotonin reuptake inhibitors and placebo in the treatment of obsessive-compulsive disorder. *American Journal of Psychiatry, 156*(9), 1409-1416.

McDougle, C. J., Goodman, W., & Price, L. H. (1994). Dopamine antagonists in tic-related and psychotic spectrum obsessive compulsive disorder. *Journal of Clinical Psychiatry, 55*(2), 24-31.

McElroy, S. L., Phillips, K. A., & Keck, P. E. (1994). Obsessive-compulsive spectrum disorder. *Journal of Clinical Psychiatry, 55*(suppl 10), 33-51.

McKay, D., Abramowitz, J. S., Calamari, J. E., Kyrios, M., Radomsky, A. S., Sookman, D., et al. (2004). A critical evaluation of obsessive-compulsive disorder subtypes: Symptoms versus mechanisms. *Clinical Psychology Review, 24*, 283-313.

McKay, D., Abramowitz, J., & Taylor, S. (2008). How should we conceptualize the obsessive compulsive spectrum? In J.S. Abramowitz, D. McKay, & S. Taylor (Eds.), *Obsessive-compulsive disorder: Subtypes and spectrum conditions (pp. 287-300)*. Oxford, UK: Elsevier.

McKay, D., Piacentini, J., Greisberg, S., Graae, F., Jaffer, M., & Miller, J. (2006). The structure of childhood obsessions and compulsions: Dimensions in an outpatient sample. *Behaviour Research and Therapy, 44*, 137-146.

Mohammadi, M. R., Ghanizadeh, A., Rahgozar, M., Noorbala, A. A., Davidian, H., Afzali, H. M., et al. (2004). Prevalence of obsessive-compulsive disorder in Iran. *BMC Psychiatry, 4*.

Murray, C. J., & Lopez, A. D. (1996). *The global burden of disease: A comprehensive assessment of mortality and disability from diseases, injuries, and risk factors in 1990 and projected to 2020*. Geneva: Harvard University Press.

Myers, J. K., Weissman, M. M., Tischler, G. L., Holzer, C. E. r., Leaf, P. J., Orvaschel, H., et al. (1984). Six-month prevalence of psychiatric disorders in three communities 1980 to 1982. *Archives of General Psychiatry, 41*(10), 959-967.

Nestadt, G., Samuels, J., Riddle, M., Bienvenu, O. J., Liang, K. Y., LaBuda, M., et al. (2000). A family study of obsessive–compulsive disorder. *Archives of General Psychiatry, 57*, 358-363.

Noshirvani, H., Kasvikis, Y., Marks, I. M., Tsakiris, F., & Monteiro, W. O. (1991). Gender-divergent aetiological factors in obsessive-compulsive disorder. *British Journal of Psychiatry, 158*, 260-263.

Obsessive-Compulsive-Cognitions-Working-Group. (1997). Cognitive assessment of obsessive-compulsive disorder. *Behaviour Research and Therapy, 35*, 667-681.

Obsessive Compulsive Cognitions Working Group. (2001). Development and initial validation of the Obsessive Beliefs Questionnaire and the Interpretation of Intrusions Inventory. *Behaviour Research and Therapy, 39*, 987-1006.

Pauls, D. L., Alsobrook, J. P., Goodman, W., Rasmussen, S. A., & Leckman, J. F. (1995). A family study of obsessive-compulsive disorder. *American Journal of Psychiatry, 152*(1), 76-84.

Peterson, B. S., Pine, D. S., Cohen, P., & Brook, J. S. (2001). Prospective, longitudinal study of tic, obsessive-compulsive, and attention-deficit/hyperactivity disorders in an epidemiological sample. *Journal of the American Academy of Child & Adolescent Psychiatry, 40*, 685-695.

Petusa, A., Fullana, M. A., Singh, S., Alonso, P., Menchon, J. M., & Mataix-Cols, D. (2008). Compulsive hoarding: OCD symptom, distinct clinical syndrome, or both? *American Journal of Psychiatry, 165*, 1289-1298.

Rachman, S. (1998). A cognitive theory of obsessions. In E. Sanavio (Ed.), *Behavior and cognitive therapy today: Essays in honor of Hans J. Eysenck* (pp. 209-222). Oxford: Elsevier Science Ltd.

Rapoport, J. L. (1990). The waking nightmare: An overview of obsessive compulsive disorder. *Journal of Clinical Psychiatry, 51*(11), 25-28.

Rasmussen, S. A., & Eisen, J. L. (1990). Epidemiology of obsessive compulsive disorder. *Journal of Clinical Psychiatry, 51*, 10-13.

Rasmussen, S. A., & Eisen, J. L. (1992). The epidemiological and clinical features of obsessive-compulsive disorder. In M. A. Jenike (Ed.), *The psychiatric clinics of North America obsessional disorders* (Vol. 15, pp. 743-758). Chicago: Saunders Company, Harcourt Brace Jovanovich, Inc.

Rasmussen, S. A., & Tsuang, M. T. (1986). DSM-III obsessive compulsive disorder: Clinical characteristics and family history. *American Journal of Psychiatry, 143*, 317-322.

Reddy, P. S., Reddy, Y. C. J., Srinath, S., Khanna, S., Sheshadri, S. P., & Girimaji, S. R. (2001). A family study of juvenile obsessive-compulsive disorder. *The Canadian Journal of Psychiatry 46*, 346-351.

Rector, N. A., Cassin, S. E., Richter, M. A., & Burroughs, E. (2009). Obsessive beliefs in first-degree relatives of patients with OCD: a test of the cognitive vulnerability model. *Journal of Anxiety Disorders, 23*(1), 145-149.

Richter, M. A., Summerfeldt, L. J., Antony, M. M., & Swinson, R. P. (2003). Obsessive– compulsive spectrum conditions in obsessive– compulsive disorder and other anxiety disorders. *Depression and Anxiety, 18*, 118-127.

Rosa-Alcazar, A. I., Sanchez-Meca, J., Gomez-Conesa, A., & F., M.-M. (2008). Psychological treatment of obsessive-compulsive disorder: A meta-analysis. *Clinical Psychology Review, 28*, 1310-1325.

Rothenberg, A. (1986). Eating disorder as a modern obsessive-compulsive syndrome. *Psychiatry, 49*(1), 45-53.

Salvoskis, P. (1985). Obsessional-compulsive problems: A cognitive-behavioural analysis. *Behaviour Research and Therapy, 23*(5), 571-583.

Samuels, J., Bienvenu, O. J., Riddle, M., Cullen, B. A., Grados, M., Liang, K. Y., et al. (2002). Hoarding in obsessive-compulsive disorder: Results from a case-control study. *Behaviour Research and Therapy, 40*, 517-528.

Sasson, Y., Zohar, J., Chopra, M., Lustig, M., Iancu, I., & Hendler, T. (1997). Epidemiology of obsessive-compulsive disorder: A world view. *Journal of Clinical Psychiatry, 58*(suppl 12), 7-10.

Saxena, S., Maidment, K. M., Vapnik, T., Golden, G., Rishwain, T., Rosen, R. M., et al. (2002). Obsessive-compulsive hoarding: symptom severity and response to multimodal treatment. *Journal of Clinical Psychiatry, 63*, 21-27.

Shavitt, R. G., Belotto, C., Curi, M., Hounie, A. G., Rosario-Campos, M. C., Diniz, J. B., et al. (2006). Clinical features associated with treatment response in obsessive-compulsive disorder. *Comprehensive Psychiatry, 47*, 276-281.

Sica, C., Novara, C., Sanavio, E., Coradeschi, D., & Dorz, S. (2002). OCD cognitions across cultures. In R. O. Frost & G. Steketee (Eds.), *Cognitive approaches to obsessions and compulsions: Theory, assessment and treatment* (pp. 371-384). Oxford: Elsevier Press.

Sica, C., Taylor, S., Arrindell, W. A., & Sanavio, E. (2006). A cross-cultural test of the cognitive theory of obsessions anc compulsions: A comparison of Greek, Italian, and American individuals: A preliminary study. *Cognitive Therapy and Research, 30*, 585-597.

Skoog, G., & Skoog, I. (1999). A 40-year follow-up of patients with obsessive–compulsive disorder *Archives of General Psychiatry, 56*, 121-127.

Stein, D. J. (2000). Neurobiology of the obsessive-compulsive spectrum disorders. *Biological Psychiatry, 47*, 296-304.

Stein, M. B., Forde, D. R., Anderson, G., & Walker, J. R. (1997). Obsessive-compulsive disorder in the community: An epidemiologic survey with clinical reappraisal. *American Journal of Psychiatry, 154*, 1120-1126.

Stein, D. J., Seedat, S., Shapira, N. A., & Goodman, W. K. (2001). Management of treatment resistant obsessive-compulsive disorder. In M. T. Pato & J. Zohar (Eds.), *Current treatments of obsessive-compulsive disorder* (2nd ed., pp. 221-237). Washington, D. C.: American Psychiatric Association Press.

Steketee, G., Frost, R. O., Bhar, S., Bouvard, M., Calamari, J., Carmin, C., et al. (2003). Psychometric validation of the Obsessive Beliefs Questionnaire and the Interpretation of Intrusions Inventory: Part I. *Behaviour Research and Therapy, 41*(8), 863-878.

Storch, E. A., Abramowitz, J., & Goodman, W. K. (2008). Where does obessive-compulsive disorder belong in DSM-V? *Depression and Anxiety, 25*, 336-347.

Summerfeldt, L. J., Richter, M. A., Antony, M. M., & Swinson, R. P. (1999). Symptom structure in obsessive–compulsive disorder: a confirmatory factor-analytic study. *Behaviour Research and Therapy, 37*(4), 297-311.

Swedo, S. E., Rapoport, J. L., Leonard, H. L., Lenane, M. C., & Cheslow, D. L. (1989). Obsessive–compulsive disorder in children and adolescents. Clinical phenomenology of 70 consecutive cases. *Archives of General Psychiatry, 46*, 335-341.

Taylor, S., McKay, D., & Abramowitz, J. S. (2005). Is obsessive-compulsive disorder a disturbance of security motivation? Comment on Szectman and Woody (2004). *Psychological Review, 112*, 650-656.

Taylor, S., Kyrios, M., Thordarson, D., Steketee, G., & Frost, R. O. (2002). Development and validation of instruments for measuring intrusions and beliefs in obsessive compulsive disorder. In R. O. Frost & G. Steketee (Eds.), *Cognitive approaches to obsessions and compulsions: Theory, assessment, and treatment* (pp. 118-138). Amsterdam, Netherlands: Pergamon/Elsevier Science Ltd.

Thomsen, P. H., & Mikkelsen, H. U. (1993). Development of personality disorders in children and adolescents with obsessive-compulsive disorder: A 6- to 22-year follow-up study. *Acta Psychiatrica Scandinavica, 87*, 456-462.

Tourette Syndrome Association International Consortium for Genetics. (2003). Obsessive-compulsive symptom dimensions in affected sibling pairs diagnosed with Gilles de la Tourette syndrome. *American Journal of Medical Genetics, 116B*(60-8).

Twohig, M. P., Hayes, S. C., & Masuda, A. (2006). Increasing Willingness to Experience Obsessions: Acceptance and Commitment Therapy as a Treatment for Obsessive-Compulsive Disorder. *Behavior Therapy, 37*, 3-13.

van Grootheest, D. S., Cath, D. C., Beekman, A. T., & Boomsma, D. I. (2005). Twin Studies on Obsessive--Compulsive Disorder: A Review. *Twin Research and Human Genetics, 8*, 450-458.

Weissman, M. M., Bland, R. C., Canino, G. J., Greenwald, S., Hwu, H. G., Lee, C. K., et al. (1994). The cross national epidemiology of obsessive compulsive disorder. The Cross National Collaborative Group. *Journal of Clinical Psychiatry, 55*, 5-10.

Wu, K. D., & Watson, D. (2003). Further investigation of the obsessive-compulsive inventory: Psychometric analysis in two non-clinical samples. *Journal of Anxiety Disorders, 17*, 305-319.

Zohar, A. H., Ratzoni, G., Pauls, D. L., Apter, A., Bleich, A., Kron, S., et al. (1992). An epidemiological study of obsessive-compulsive disorder and related disorders in Israeli adolescents. *Journal of the American Academy of Child & Adolescent Psychiatry, 31*, 1057-1061.

Chapter 2

COGNITIVE DEFICITS ASSOCIATED WITH OCD

ABSTRACT

Biological models of OCD have suggested an underlying brain dysfunction, centred primarily in the orbital frontal cortex and basal ganglia. As a consequence, many studies have been conducted to discover possible neurobiological deficits associated with OCD. In this chapter we reviewed the most recent research examining neuropsychological test data on OCD. We considered neuropsychological evidences linked to: (1) different cognitive functions, (2) different OCD manifestations (subtypes), (3) comparisons between OCD and other types of patients (e.g., depressed or anxious ones), and (4) comparisons between OCD treated and not treated.

Current evidences suggest the presence of executive function deficits in OCD, particularly in response inhibition and planning; whether such deficits are trait-related (independent of symptomatology) or state-dependent (dependent on symptomatology) warrants more research. Likewise, it is not clear to what extent these deficits are alleviated with traditional behaviour therapy (exposure with response prevention) or medication (selective serotonin reuptake inhibitors).

INTRODUCTION

Obsessive-Compulsive Disorder (OCD) has been extensively studied in the last decade, with increased emphasis on its biological substrates. Evidence from a variety of sources suggests that OCD may involve underlying brain dysfunction, particularly in the orbital frontal cortex and basal ganglia (Cottraux & Gerard, 1998; Insel, 1992; Purcell, Maruff, Kyrios & Pantelis, 1998a; Saxena, Brody, Schwartz & Baxter, 1998; Stein, 2002). In fact, abnormal feedback loops within cortical-striatal-thalamic circuits have been hypothesized to play a key role in the pathophysiology of OCD (Alexander, DeLong & Strick, 1986; Baxter et al., 1992; Kwon et al, 2003; Rapoport & Wise, 1988; Rosenberg & Keshavan, 1998). For instance, structural imaging studies revealed that orbital frontal cortex and basal ganglia volumes are smaller among patients with OCD than in normal controls (Robinson et al., 1995; Szeszko et al., 1999) and research using functional imaging techniques indicates that the same regions are abnormally activated in OCD individuals (Baxter et al., 1987; Saxena et al., 1999). In addition, neurologic syndromes that affect the basal ganglia and frontal cortex (e.g., striopallidodentate mineralizations, closed head injuries, Pick's disease) are associated with development of OCD-like symptoms (Ames, Cummings, Wirshing, Quinn & Mahler, 1994; Tonkonogy, Smith & Barreira, 1994), whereas neurosurgical disruption of orbital/prefrontal-basal ganglia circuits significantly decreases OCD symptoms in patients who were refractory to either CBT or SSRI interventions (Mindus, Rasmussen & Lindquist, 1994). It has also been proposed that patients with focal brain lesions (acquired OCD) and patients with idiopathic OCD may share a structural damage to specific frontal-limbic-subcortical circuits (Berthier, Kulisevsky, Gironell & Heras, 1996). Some studies showed that OCD patients had electroencephalographic abnormalities in the frontal-temporal regions (Jenike & Brotman, 1984) and increased frequency of neurologic soft signs associated with basal ganglia dysfunction (Hollander et al, 1990). Lastly, deficits in executive functions in individuals with Tourette Syndrome and co-morbid OCD provide further evidence for a substantial impairment of the frontal-striatal-thalamic-frontal circuit as underlying symptoms of Tourette's syndrome with co-morbid OCD (Muller et al., 2003; Watkins et al., 2005). Collectively, this research has lead to the proposal that OCD arises from a disruption in a brain level fear circuitry (discussed in Abramowitz, Taylor, & McKay, in press).

In sum, neurobiological models of OCD cannot be ignored in building a thorough explanation of this complex and severe disorder. In the following sections we therefore will try to illustrate the neurobiological functioning in OCD by considering the main findings emerging from neuropsychological test data.

2.1. Neuropsychological Test Data

It has been hypothesized that impairments in motor inhibition and cognitive flexibility may be central deficits in OCD (Chamberlain, Blackwell, Fineberg, Robbins, & Sahakian, 2005). These deficits putatively reflect a reduced capacity of patients with OCD to inhibit intrusive or ritualistic cognitions and motor response tendencies. Accordingly, many studies have been conducted to discover possible neuropsychological deficits associated with OCD (Cottraux & Gerard, 1998; Purcell, et al., 1998a). Examinations of neuropsychological functioning in OCD have been also justified by a variety of clinical observations. For example, although the majority of individuals with OCD report that they recognize the senselessness of their obsessions, they are still compelled to engage in rituals or cannot dismiss the obsessional idea. Such phenomena may be linked to impaired functioning in the frontal lobes and executive functioning (Lezak, 1995). Moreover, the differences between 'normal' and 'OCD' cognitions are that the latter are more frequent, more intense, and elicit more resistance and subjective discomfort; as a consequence, OCD may be well characterized in terms of failures to inhibit, or shift attention from, these ongoing thoughts towards other more pleasant, or less distressing, cognitions.

In the present section we review the key neuropsychological findings that have clinical salience and provides a cognitive profile of OCD, paying attention to: (1) different cognitive functions, (2) different OCD manifestations (subtypes), (3) comparisons between OCD and other types of patients (e.g., depressed or anxious ones), and (4) comparisons between OCD treated and not treated.

Memory

Memory has been an important area of investigation in light of the persistent complaint among individuals with OCD that they doubt the accuracy or completeness of their actions. To illustrate, individuals who check the stove do so because of uncertainty that it was done, not that there is a strong belief that it was not done at all. This has stimulated a large body of literature, although much of it has not been supportive of a memory deficit hypothesis (e.g., Boone, Ananth, Philpott, Kaur, & Djenderjian, 1991; Christensen, Kim, Dysken, & Hoover, 1992; Dirson, Bouvard, Cottraux, & Martin, 1995; Radomsky & Rachman, 1999; Sher, Frost, Kushner, Crews, & Alexander,

1989; Zielinski, Taylor, & Juzwin, 1991). Other authors have noted that repetitive checking behaviour may suggest attention problems or a failure to appropriately encode memories for self-actions. However, studies indexing reality monitoring and memory for self-actions in OCD patients failed to find evidence of impairments in these areas (Constans, Foa, Franklin, & Mathews, 1995; Hermans, Martens, De Cort, Pieters, & Eelen, 2003; McNally & Kohlbeck, 1993).

There have also been suggestions that a central problems in OCD is at the metamemory level. Several studies showed that OCD checkers seem less confident in their memory judgements (McNally & Kohlbeck, 1993; Tolin et al., 2001; Woods, Vevea, Chambless & Bayen, 2002). Importantly, this lack of confidence was evident from both self-report measures regarding confidence ratings and by the slower reaction times on the part of checkers (MacDonald, Antony, MacLeod, & Richter, 1997). It is also important to note that it is possible that subclinical obsessive–compulsive individuals check in response to accurate appraisals of memory impairment, while OCD checkers check in response to doubts that are related to their OCD symptoms rather than to actual deficits in memory (see MacDonald et al., 1997).

OCD may involve other types of memory impairment. Consistent with this possibility, several neuropsychological investigations have found that OCD patients show impairments in non-verbal episodic memory (Boone et al., 1991; Christensen et al., 1992; Deckersbach, Otto, Savage, Baer & Jenike, 2000; Dirson, Bouvard, Cottraux & Martin, 1995; Martinot et al., 1990; Purcell et al., 1998a; Savage et al., 1996; Savage et al., 1999; Zielinski et al., 1991). Other studies found impairment in recall performance on tasks such as the *Rey Complex Figure Test* (RCFT; Osterrieth, 1944) and the *Benton Visual Retention Test* (BVRT; Benton, 1974). It has been argued that this impairment is due to inappropriate or/and slow organizational strategies (Kuelz, Hohagen, & Voderholzer, 2004; Martinot et al., 1990; Savage et al., 1999; Savage & Rauch, 2000; Deckersbach et al., 2000; Kim, Park, Shin & Kwon, 2002; Shin et al., 2004).

In sum, no consistent support for a general memory deficit for verbal information has been found, whereas some studies support the idea of a metamemory deficit. Memory impairments for experimentally presented non-verbal (particularly visual) stimuli have been more frequently demonstrated. A possible explanation for this pattern of results is that non-verbal memory is more susceptible than verbal memory to executive impairment (i.e., impaired encoding strategies) due to its more abstract nature and increased demands on organizational capacity (Moritz et al., 2005; Savage et al., 1999; see Greisberg

& McKay, 2003, for a review). Actually, patients with OCD have been demonstrated to be less likely to use spontaneously generated organizational strategies during verbal episodic memory and visuoconstruction tasks. However, whether this organizational deficit is generalized to other areas of cognitive functioning is questioned (Moritz et al., 2005; Roth, Milovan, Baribeau, O'Connor & Todorov, 2004).

Executive Functioning

Studies on executive functions have produced inconsistent results when applied to individuals with OCD. In some studies, OCD patients demonstrated impaired performance on general tests of executive functions (Deckersbach et al., 2000; Head, Bolton & Hymas, 1989; Purcell et al., 1998b; Veale, Sahakian, Owen & Marks, 1996), but in others studies these deficits did not emerge (Abbruzzese, Bellodi, Ferri and Scarone, 1995; Schmidtke, Schorb, Winkelmann & Hohagen, 1998; Zielinski et al., 1991). The lack of support for the hypothesis regarding executive functioning is surprising in light of the central place of brain areas long associated with this particular cognitive function in fear circuitry models of OCD. Further, whereas some studies of sustained attention among individuals with OCD showed below average performance for sustained attention (Schmidtke, Schorb, Winkelmann & Hohagen, 1998; Veale et al., 1996) others failed to identify these results (Boone et al., 1991; Milliery, Bouvard, Aupetit & Cottraux, 2000). Therefore, the research reviewed to this point fails to persuasively point to either a memory or executive dysfunction in the aetiology of OCD. There is, however, limited research to suggest that the interaction between executive and memory functioning may serve as a basis for explaining this problem. Research has shown that individuals with OCD has difficulty organizing their memories (as shown in *RCFT* performance; Savage et al., 1999).

Attention Bias

The clinical symptoms of OCD are suggestive of processing biases, such as fixations with potential contamination sources or stimuli that would not normally evoke emotional responses. Modified Stroop tasks have been used to study attentional biases to threatening information in OCD. In a modified Stroop task, participants see emotionally laden words (e.g., toilet) presented in different colors and are instructed to name the color, while at the same time, attempting to ignore their semantic content.

Foa, Ilai, McCarthy, Shoyer, and Murdock (1993) administered a modified Stroop task to 23 individuals with OCD with washing rituals (washers), 10 OCD patients without washing rituals (non-washers) and 14 normal participants. Results indicated that compared to non-washers and controls, washers evidenced longer latencies for colour-naming contamination words (threat information specific to their fear). In contrast, OCD non-washers showed interference to general threat words compared to washers and controls. Thus, these results demonstrate that selective processing of threat information in OCD might be highly specific to the patient's particular concerns.

Lavy, van Oppen, and van den Hout (1994) found specific attentional biases in OCD. They found that 33 individuals with OCD selectively attended to threat words related to obsessions and compulsions compared to normal controls. Importantly, patients with OCD did not exhibit interference effects to positive words related to obsessions and compulsions or to negative threatening words in general.

Direnfeld, Pato, and Roberts (2001) assessed attentional bias in a heterogeneous sample of individuals with OCD (n = 42) over the course of a 12-week exposure and ritual prevention group treatment. Attentional bias decreased significantly from pre- to post-treatment and participants who no longer experienced an attentional bias at treatment termination reported fewer total numbers of obsessive symptoms. These results indicate that interference is reduced as these symptoms are ameliorated through treatment.

It is important to note that a number of observations have challenged the interpretation of Stroop interference in that exaggerated interference effects in the presence of threatening distracters does not necessarily mean that these anxious individuals were selectively encoding the threatening distracter. For example, people who score high on questionnaire measures of "repression," a personality trait that has been assumed to reflect the avoidance of processing of aversive information, also take a longer time to color name threat words relative to neutral-emotional words on the emotional Stroop task information (Dawkins & Furnham, 1989;MacLeod, 1996; Muller & Roberts, 2005). The visual dot-probe task (MacLeod, Mathews, & Tata, 1986) seems less vulnerable to the interpretative concerns associated with the modified Stroop task (Muller & Roberts, 2005). In this task, MacLeod and colleagues (1986) observed that anxious participants were faster than controls in responding to the probe when it was in the exact location of threat-related words. Anxious individuals' increased speed for detecting probes appearing in the vicinity of threat stimuli has been replicated across a number of studies (e.g., MacLeod & Mathews, 1988; Mogg, Mathews, & Eysenck, 1992; Mogg, Millar, & Bradley, 2000). A potential explanation for such findings may be because anxious participants were directing their attention disproportionately towards the threat location (anxious individuals demonstrated vigilance for threatening information). In contrast, normal participants tended to direct their attention away from the threat information suggesting that these individuals were avoiding threatening information. Tata, Leibowitz, Prunty, Cameron, and Pickering (1996) demonstrated that patients with OCD are also characterized by a bias in selective attention for threat-related information using the dot-probe task.

In summary, the reported findings suggest that patients with OCD selectively attend to threatening information, particularly information related to their particular concerns. Such biases in attention may lead to the overrepresentation of threat cues within the information that participants encode from their environment, contributing to the development and maintenance of intrusive obsessive thoughts in OCD.

Set-Shifting

Set-shifting involves the ability to switch attention from one aspect of a stimulus to another in an ongoing task, in accordance with changing reinforcement contingencies. Given the perseveration and repetition pertaining to clinical picture, set-shifting impairments should be a core feature of the neurocognitive profile of OCD. Typically, set-shifting abilities have been studied through the Wisconsin Card Sorting Task (WCST) or the Cambridge Automated Neuropsychological Test Battery (CANTAB). While some studies have identified set-shifting deficits in OCD (Head et al., 1989; Malloy, 1987; Veale et al., 1996; Gambini, Abbruzzese & Scarone, 1993, Hymas, Lees, Bolton, Epps & Head, 1991; Bannon, Gonsalvez, Croft & Boyce, 2006; Lawrence et al., 2006), other studies did not find such deficits (Christensen et al., 1992; Moritz et al., 2001, 2002, Roth et al., 2004; Nielen and Den Boer, 2003; Purcell et al., 1998b; Zielinski et al., 1991).

Purcell et al. (1998b) argued that inconsistency on set-shifting tasks with OCD patients may be attributed to sample heterogeneity and a lack of control of co-morbid disorders. Moreover, the expression of set-shifting deficits in OCD may be related to clinical disease severity or disease progression (Chamberlain et al., 2005; Nielen and Den Boer, 2003). Actually, studies that excluded patients with high depression severity scores have mostly shown that set-shifting performance is unimpaired in OCD (Boone et al., 1991; Purcell et al., 1998b) whereas investigations that did not control for depressive symptoms have reported such dysfunctions (Cox, Fedio, & Rapoport, 1989; Moritz, Kloss, Katenkamp, Birkner, & Hand, 1999).

Response Inhibition

The term 'response inhibition' (RI) refers to cognitive processes enabling executive control over pre-potent motor responses in accordance with changing situational demands (e.g., Aron, Fletcher, Bullmore, Sahakianb & Robbins, 2003; Logan, Cowan, & Davis, 1984). The orbitofrontal-subcortical pathways are thought to produce the response inhibition and therefore the inhibition may be the most vulnerable of various attention tasks by OCD subjects. Initial evidence for RI deficits in OCD came from studies using oculomotor tasks that required the suppression of eye movements. Failures of inhibition were identified in treatment naïve children and adults with OCD (Rosenberg et al., 1997; Rosenberg, Dick, O'Hearn, & Sweeney, 1997).

In Go/No-Go tasks, subjects are required to make a simple motor response (such as pressing a button) as quickly as possible when target stimuli are presented, and withhold the response when non-target stimuli are presented. Bannon, Gonsalvez, Croft and Boyce (2002) found that OCD patients made significantly more commission errors than matched panic disorder subjects in a computerised task necessitating the inhibition of responses on a proportion of trials (OCD patients tended to make inappropriate motor responses to non-target stimuli). Aycicegi, Dinn, Harris and Erkmen (2003) identified impaired performance on conflict blocks in OCD individuals compared to healthy matched controls, consistent with Bannon and associates' findings. Penadés et al. (2007) tested 27 patients who met DSM-IV criteria for OCD and 25 age, handedness and IQ-matched healthy control subjects in the Go/No-Go, Stop and motor Stroop tasks. OCD patients performed significantly worse than controls in the selective inhibition of their motor responses (Go/No-Go) and in the inhibition of cognitive interference (Stroop), and also showed worse performance in suppressing previously triggered motor responses (Stop).

Similar deficits have been identified in Tourette's syndrome complicated by co-morbid OCD (Muller et al., 2003). Watkins et al. (2005) utilised a computerised Go/No-Go task in which response contingencies were reversed on some blocks of trials. This enabled the quantification of switching cost, in terms of reduction in correct responding on reversal blocks. They found that the OCD group had an abnormally high switching cost compared to both matched healthy controls and volunteers with Tourette's syndrome.

Lastly, Chamberlain et al. (2007) administered the Intradimensional/Extradimensional Shift, Stop-Signal, and Cambridge Gamble tasks to 20 unaffected first-degree relatives, 20 OCD patient probands with washing/checking symptoms, and 20 healthy matched comparison subjects without a family history of OCD. Results showed that unaffected first-degree relatives and OCD patient probands showed cognitive inflexibility (extradimensional set shifting) and motor impulsivity (stop-signal reaction times). Decision making (Cambridge Gamble task) was intact. Bannon et al. (2006) have proposed that deficit in RI is trait-like in nature. In other words, such deficit would not be dependent of symptomatology.

Working Memory

Individuals with OCD perform poorly on tasks that engage spatial working memory, when task difficulty is high (i.e., a high workload; Purcell et al., 1998a; 1998b). From the neuropsychological findings it is not clear whether at higher load levels the working memory system is physiologically dysfunctional (i.e., has a physical basis), or whether working memory is intact, but somehow disrupted by other processes (i.e., is intact but is utilized inefficiently).

Martin, Wiggs, Altemus, Rubenstein, & Murphy (1995) tested OCD patients and normal subjects (n = 18 per group) on a self-paced, working memory task that is largely mediated by the prefrontal cortex. The OCD participants had normal working memory spans and normal recognition memory for all types of material tested (abstract words, common objects, and novel nonsense objects). The patients, however, were slower than the comparison participants, and the time they took to complete the tasks was significantly correlated with ratings of OCD symptoms (r = .539, p<.05) and depression (r = .643, p <.01), but not anxiety. Slowed performance on this self-paced task was discussed in relation to normal response times by OCD patients under typical laboratory conditions. It was suggested that this discrepancy may be related to a broader dissociation between real-world and laboratory performance as seen in some patients with prefrontal lobe dysfunction.

Van der Wee and colleagues (2003) conducted a f MRI study in 11 treatment-free female patients with OCD and 11 for sex-, age-, education-, and handedness matched healthy controls in order to assess performance on a parametric spatial *n*-back task as well as the underlying neuronal substrate and its dynamics. Patients with OCD performed poorly at the highest level of task difficulty and engaged the same set of brain regions as the matched healthy controls. In this set, the effect of difficulty on magnitude of brain activity was the same in patients and in controls except for a region covering the anterior cingulate cortex. In this region activity was significantly elevated in patients with OCD at all levels of the parametric task.

Recently, Nakao et al. (2009) conducted a neuropsychological and fMRI study on 40 drug-free OCD patients and 25 age- sex ratio- and handedness ratio- healthy controls. A neuropsychological battery (WAIS-R, WMS-R, R-OCFT and WCST) was administered and 0-, 2- back task was required. The patients showed a significantly greater activation in several regions including right dorsolateral prefrontal cortex, left superior temporal gyrus, insula and cuneus compared to healthy controls, indicating a visual working memory dysfunction. In contrast with Van der Wee et al. (2003), the effect of difficulty on magnitude of ACC activity was not found, probably because of differences on N-back task that in study conducted by Nakao et al. was simpler. These findings do not provide evidence for a deficit of the spatial working memory system proper, but suggest that the abnormal performance pattern may be secondary to another aspect of executive dysfunction in OCD.

Planning

Some studies evidenced pure planning deficits in OCD (Bannon et al., 2006; Purcell et al. 1998a, 1998b; Veale et al., 1996) but these deficits did not emerge in other researches (Cavedini, Cisima, Riboldi, D'Annucci & Bellodi, 2002; Nielen & Den Boer, 2003). Some patients showed abnormal psychomotor slowing (as indexed by lengthened latency/thinking times compared to controls) to planning tasks such as the Tower of London. It may be that lengthened latency times are consequential to strategy failures, attention problems, and/or chronic doubting in situations where the subjects are informed via computer feedback that they have just made an error (Chamberlain et al., 2005).

2.2. Cognitive Deficits Across OCD Subtypes

Obsessive–compulsive disorder (OCD) is clinically heterogeneous. Factor analytic studies have consistently identified distinct but potentially overlapping symptom dimensions within OCD, which can coexist in the same patients and are stable over time (Mataix-Cols, Marks, Greist, Kobak & Baer 2002; McKay ct al., 2004). It may be that the different aspects of this disorder are associated with different neuropsychological deficits; it is also possible that several neural mechanisms are involved in mediating the different OCD symptom dimensions (e.g., Mataix-Cols et al., 2004).

Research investigating distinctive neuropsychological features across symptom-based OCD subtypes has focused mainly on patients with checking rituals (e.g., Sher, Frost, & Otto, 1983; Tallis, Pratt & Jamani, 1999; Zitterl et al., 2001), although less common subtypes, such as hoarding (Wincze, 2001) and obsessional slowness (Hymas et al.,1991) have also been investigated. Compared to non-checkers, checkers tended to exhibit (a) deficits in general memory and memory for actions (Sher, Frost, Kushner, Crews, & Alexander, 1989; Sher et al., 1983; Sher, Mann, & Frost, 1984); and (b) deficits in memory confidence (Zitterl et al., 2001). Actually, many authors have reported that memory deficits in people with OCD are more related to compulsive checking than compulsive washing (Bouvard, Dirson, & Cottraux, 1997; MacDonald et al., 1997; Omori et al., 2007; Rubenstein, Peynircioglu, Chambless, & Pigott, 1993; Sher et al., 1989; Sher et al., 1984).

However, recent findings suggested that checkers may have memory confidence problems not due to primary memory deficits but to meta-memory impairment (Omori et al., 2007). Another explanation has to do with the observed association between inhibition and general memory in checkers (Enright, Beech & Claridge, 1995; Hoenig, Hochrein, Muller & Wagner, 2002; Omori et al., 2007). Actually, the ability to respond effectively and recall prior information depends, in part, on the capacity to ignore or inhibit irrelevant information and to focus on the task at hand. One plausible explanation for poorer inhibition among checkers is that checkers also had poorer memory scores, which in turn may be due to interference effects resulting from a failure to inhibit irrelevant or distracting material.

Another approach to examine possible differences across OCD subtypes has been to make direct comparisons of performance on standardized neuropsychological tests. Abbruzzese et al., (1993) failed to find memory differences among OCD subtypes on the revised Wechsler Memory Scale-Revised (WMS-R; Wechsler, 1987). Abbruzzese et al., (1995) examined performance on the WCST in 33 OCD patients and matched controls. They found no differences among various OCD subtypes, classified according to YBOCS-SC responses (checkers, washers, mental checkers, and mixed cohorts). Kyrios, Wainwright, Purcell, Pantelis, and Maruff (1999) compared neuropsychological performance of OCD subtypes on the CANTAB, an advanced computerised cognitive testing battery. Fifty-nine OCD patients were categorized into (a) washers; (b) checkers; (c) obsessives; and (d) others or mixed symptom profile, according the YBOCS-SC. Comparisons among washers, checkers, and obsessives revealed few neuropsychological differences between these subtypes. Also Simpson and colleagues (2006) found that self-reported OCD symptom dimensions, including hoarding, were not significantly related to performance on neuropsychological tasks of executive functioning, nonverbal memory, and motor speed.

On the contrary, Lawrence et al. (2006) found that OCD patients with high hoarding symptoms performed worse than patients with low hoarding symptoms and healthy controls on the *Iowa Gambling Task* (IGT; Bechara, Damasio, Damasio, & Anderson, 1994). Moreover, Lawrence and colleagues (2006) showed that the symmetry/hoarding dimension was moderately associated with poorer set-shifting ability on the WCST and, in particular, with a greater number of perseverative errors and a lower number of categories completed. Hoarders have problems in decision-making, indeed (Frost & Gross, 1993; Steketee & Frost, 2003). It is important to note, however, that recent research raises questions about whether hoarding symptoms represent a “pure” dimension of OCD or a separate type of mental health problem (Grisham, Brown, Liverant & Campbell-Sills, 2005).

Some studies used a dimensional approach by examining correlations between neuropsychological performance and ratings on subscales of symptoms subtypes. For instance, Mataix-Cols et al. (1999) found that poorer performance on a planning task positively correlated with checking symptoms in a sub clinical OCD cohort. However, these findings have not been replicated, and there have been few investigations of this kind (i.e., Kyrios et al., 1999).

2.3. OCD And Other Clinical Disorders: Are Neuropsychological Performances Different?

Thirty patients with OCD, 30 with panic disorder, 20 with unipolar depression, and 30 controls completed a computerized neuropsychological battery that assessed the accuracy and latency of executive functions (Purcell et al., 1998b). Patients with OCD, compared to the other groups, were impaired on measures of spatial working memory, spatial recognition, and motor initiation and execution.

Aycicegi et al., (2003) administered a comprehensive neuropsychological battery along with measures of schizotypal personality and depression to patients with OCD and matched healthy controls. OCD patients demonstrated performance deficits on measures of delayed memory, response inhibition, alternation learning, and obtained significantly higher scores on measures of disinheriting, impulsivity, and temporolimbic symptoms; however, OCD patients did not exhibit impaired performance on tests of executive function and verbal fluency, and did not report a significantly greater number of problems in executive functioning, when depressive and schizotypal symptoms were taken into account.

Part of the inconsistency of the neuropsychological studies of OCD may be due to the lack of control of co-morbid depression (Basso, Bornstein, Carona & Morton, 2001). Depressive symptomatology is also associated with executive function deficits (Franke et al., 1993; Martin, Huber, Rief & Exner, 2008; Martin, Oren & Boone, 1991), and many individuals with OCD develop concurrent depression during their lifetime (Rasmussen & Eisen, 1991). Moreover, functional imaging data suggest differential patterns of activation between patients with OCD with and without depression (Baxter et al., 1989)

Basso et al. (2001) found that executive function deficits are less strongly associated with OCD than with comorbid depressive symptomatology. Moritz et al., (2001) provided direct evidence that set-shifting performance, as assessed with the WCST, is disturbed in OCD patients with elevated depression scores. In their study, patients with low depressive symptomatology and healthy control subjects did not significantly differ regarding WCST performance. In another study, Moritz, Heeren, Andresen and Krausz, (2001) provided evidence that the mediating effect of depression on neuropsychological disturbances in OCD extended to mnestic dysfunctions; depressed patients showed severe memory dysfunctions in recall task of the

Rey Figure and *Corsi Block Tapping*. However, independently of co-morbid depressive symptoms, visuospatial transformation was disturbed in OCD (Moritz et al., 2001).

Moritz et al., (2002) investigated whether schizophrenic, unipolar depressive, and obsessive–compulsive psychiatric patients show a distinguishable profile in tasks considered sensitive to frontal lobe functioning - deficits in verbal working memory (digit span backward), interference/ distractibility (Stroop task), concept formation/problem solving (WCST), verbal fluency (creativity task), and set-shifting (Trail-Making Test). Healthy controls showed better performance relative to depressive and schizophrenic patients who exhibited comparable deficits in all tasks. OCD patients revealed dysfunctions in set-shifting and in fluency task. Dysfunctions in domains of working memory, verbal fluency, distractibility, and concept formation were not confined to a specific psychiatric population and they may therefore represent a more general rather than a special vulnerability to psychiatric illness.

Recently, Martin et al.(2008) investigated the specificity of cognitive impairments in 19 subjects with OCD, 19 patients with schizophrenia and 19 matched healthy controls. A full range neuropsychological assessment was administered in order to get information on several cognitive domains (working memory, verbal memory, simple attention, complex attention, visual spatial skills, flexibility of the executive functions and concept formation). Subjects with OCD and subjects with schizophrenia evidenced a notable parallelism, showing significant differences compared to healthy controls in visual memory, verbal memory and simple attention tasks. Specifically patients with schizophrenia showed a significantly greater impairment in simple attention. However, all significant differences that were found between OC subjects and control subjects disappeared after controlling for depression

2.4. Neuropsychological Performance and Treatment

In a study by Nielen and Den Boer (2003), 19 individuals with OCD were tested before and after treatment with fluoxetine. Before entering the treatment phase, OCD individuals and 24 healthy controls underwent a series of cognitive tasks concerning several executive functions through the CANTAB. Compared to healthy controls, OCD patients displayed impairments in planning ability, spatial working memory and motor speed that persisted after clinical improvement. These data suggest that cognitive impairments in OCD are not secondary to symptoms and therefore may form a trait feature of the disorder. Further, Kim, Park, Shin and Kwon (2002) demonstrated that successfully treated individuals with OCD continued to exhibit cognitive deficits in nonverbal memory, initiation of spontaneous or self-guided thought/action and controlled attention, despite their significant improvement. Bannon et al., (2006) examined executive functions (set shifting, inhibition, planning, verbal fluency and working memory) in 60 participants (20 actively symptomatic OCD, 20 remitted OCD and 20 Panic Disorder). OCD patients showed deficits in inhibition and set shifting c compared to Panic Disorder controls; whereas, no deficits emerged in planning, verbal fluency or working memory. In another study, the authors reassessed a sub sample of OCD individuals (participants in Study 1) once they reached remitted status. The second study found that the identified executive function deficits in individuals were stable over time and remained unchanged despite symptom recovery. In contrast, Kuelz et al., (2006) found that cognitive strategies and cognitive dysfunction in OCD can improve with cognitive behavioural treatment; such intervention would enable OCD patients to think and act in a more flexible way.

Recently, Andrés et al. (2008) conducted research on cognitive dysfunction on children and adolescents with OCD after treatment. A neuropsychological battery (immediate and delayed memory, immediate visual memory, speed of information processing, inhibition of response and categorization) was administered to 29 patients (7-18 years old) and 22 healthy subjects age-, sex- and intellectual level matched. The assessment was conducted before and after a naturalistic treatment (all subjects with OCD were pharmacologically treated and 19 patients received a cognitive-behavioural treatment). After 6 months of treatment the profile of OCD group was normalized with the exception of a worse performance by OCD group on immediate and delayed recall of verbal memory. Although these results are in contrast with previously quoted studies on cognitive dysfunctions stability in adults with OCD in recovery, these differences could be explained by very early onset and time of evolution of OCD.

Conclusion

Greisberg and McKay (2003) were amongst the first researchers to suggest that cognitive deficits in people with OCD are most consistently found on tests requiring the use of organizational strategies in conjunction with short and long term memory. It is possible that most, if not all, of the memory deficits reported in OCD could be accounted for by non-mnemonic processing failures, in particular the rigid implementation of inappropriate strategies (Deckersbach et al., 2000; Kim et al., 2002; Kuelz et al., 2004; Martinot et al., 1990; Savage et al., 1999; Savage and Rauch, 2000).

In fact, current research suggests the presence of executive function deficits in OCD, particularly in response inhibition and planning; whether such deficits are trait-related (independent of symptomatology) or state-dependent (dependent on symptomatology) warrants more research (Bannon et al., 2006). Likewise, it is not clear to what extent these deficits are alleviated with traditional behaviour therapy (exposure with response prevention) or medication (selective serotonin reuptake inhibitors). Of course, should cognitive impairments in OCD be not secondary to symptoms, it would be possible to conclude more firmly that such disorder involves a basic deficit in some processes such as executive functions.

It does appear from the research that individuals with OCD experience difficulties in memory. However, as we have seen, the memory deficits appear less to do with memory per se, but the degree of organization necessary to effectively complete the task. That is, when presented with tasks demanding recall under well-structured circumstances, OCD patients perform in a manner similar to those without OCD. When tasks are less clearly defined, or when the ability to recall information is predicated on a combination of memory and organization, then significant impairment becomes evident. For instance, the most consistent findings in OCD have emerged from a relatively short and narrow focused measure of the interaction between memory and executive functioning, the RCFT (reviewed in Greisberg & McKay, 2003). The nonverbal memory deficit in OCD patients may be related to the impairment of the organizational process of memory, which is known to be mediated by the prefrontal-striate system. Neuroimaging findings (see below) have indeed showed that the prefrontal-striatal system is related to the pathophysiology of OCD. Lastly, OCD patients are also characterized by a bias in selective attention for threat-related information (e.g. Tata et al., 1996). These deficits might suggest executive function deficits too (e.g., fixation or attentional deficit).

No others neuropsychological functions resulted consistently impaired in OCD individuals. Moreover, research on OCD subtypes (excluding hoarding symptoms) did not confirm that the different aspects of this disorder are associated with different neuropsychological deficits. Looking at inconsistent results obtained on OCD subtypes, it is important to bear in mind that neuropsychological tasks may be open to diverse influences, such as metamemory (Gershuny & Sher, 1995). Radomsky and Rachman (1999), for example, found better memory for ''contaminated'' than ''noncontaminated'' objects in a sample of OCD ''washers.'' A similar pattern of threat-relevant memory bias was demonstrated in a sample of OCD ''checkers'' (Radomsky, Rachman & Hammond, 2001).

It may be also that some differences would emerge by taking in consideration other features of the disorder. For instance, the age of OCD onset may play a role in the kind of impairment in obsessive-compulsive symptom. Roth, Milovan, Baribeau and O'Connor (2005) found that patients with early onset of OCD showed a few signs of performance deficits in various neuropsychological tasks, whereas individuals with late OCD onset had poorer performance on verbal and visual memory, executive functions and auditory attention. It has been in fact hypothesized a "primary" subtype of the disorder, characterized by late onset and frontal systems dysfunction (Blanes & McGuire, 1997; see also, Busatto et al., 2001).

References

Abbruzzese, M., Bellodi, L., Ferri, S., & Scarone, S. (1993). Memory functioning in obsessive-compulsive disorder. *Behavioural Neurology, 6*(3), 119-122.

Abbruzzese, M., Bellodi, L., Ferri, S., & Scarone, S. (1995). Frontal lobe dysfunction in schizophrenia and obsessive-compulsive disorder: A neuropsychological study. *Brain and Cognition, 27*(2), 202-212.

Abramowitz, J. S., Taylor, S., & McKay, D. (in press). Obsessive-compulsive disorder. *The Lancet.*

Alexander, G. E., DeLong, M. R., & Strick, P. L. (1986). Parallel organization of functionally segregated circuits linking basal ganglia and cortex. *Annual Review of Neuroscience, 9*, 357-381.

Ames, D., Cummings, J. L., Wirshing, W. C., Quinn, B., & Mahler, M. (1994). Repetitive and compulsive bahavior in frontal lobe degenarations. *Journal of Neuropsychiatry and Clinical Neurosciences, 6*(2), 100-113.

Andres, S., Lazaro, L., Salamero, M., Boget, T., Penades, R., & Castro-Fornieles, J. (2008). Changes in cognitive dysfunction in children and adolescents with obsessive-compulsive disorder after treatment. *Journal of Psychiatric Research, 42*, 507-514.

Aron, A. R., Fletcher, P. C., Bullmore, E. T., Sahakian, B. J., & Robbins, T. W. (2003). Stop-signal inhibition disrupted by damage to right inferior frontal gyrus in humans. *Nature Neuroscience, 6*(2), 115-116.

Aycicegi, A., Dinn, W. M., Harris, C. L., & Erkmen, H. (2003). Neuropsychological function in obsessive-compulsive disorder: Effects of comorbid conditions on task performance. *European Psychiatry, 18*(5), 241-248.

Bannon, S., Gonsalvez, C. J., Croft, R. J., & Boyce, P. M. (2002). Response inhibition deficits in obsessive-compulsive disorder. *Psychiatry Research, 110*(2), 165-174.

Bannon, S., Gonsalvez, C. J., Croft, R. J., & Boyce, P. M. (2006). Executive functions in obsessive-compulsive disorder: Strate or trait deficits? *Australian and New Zeland Journal of Psychiatry, 40*(11-12), 1031-1038.

Basso, M. R., Bornstein, R. A., Carona, F., & Morton, R. (2001). Depression accounts for executive function deficits in obsessive-compulsive disorder. *Neuropsychiatry, Neuropsychology and Behavioural Neurology, 14*(4), 241-245.

Baxter, L. R., Phelps, M. D., Mazziotta, J. C., Guze, B. H., Schwartz, J. M., & Selin, C. E. (1987). Local cerebral glucose metabolic rates in obsessive-compulsive disorder: A comparison with rates in unipolar depression and in normal controls. *Archives of General Psychiatry, 44*(3), 211-218.

Baxter, L. R., Schwartz, J. M., Berman, K. S., Szuba, M. P., Guze, B. H., Mazziotta, J. C., et al. (1992). Caudate glucose metabolite changes with both drug and behavior therapy for obsessive-compulsive disorder. *Archives of General Psychiatry, 49*(9), 681-689.

Baxter, L. R., Schwartz, J. M., Phelps, M. D., Mazziotta, J. C., Guze, B. H., Selin, C. E., et al. (1989). Reduction of prefrontal cortex glucose metabolism common to three types of depression. *Archives of General Psychiatry, 46*(3), 243-250.

Bechara, A., Damasio, A. R., Damasio, H., & Anderson, S. W. (1994). Insensitivity to future consequences following damage to human prefrontal cortex. *Cognition, 50*(1-3), 7-15.

Benton, A. (1974). *Revised Visual Retention Test* (IV ed.). San Antonio, TX: The Psychological Corporation.

Berthier, M. L., Kulisevsky, J., Gironell, A., & Heras, J. A. (1996). Obsessive-compulsive disorder associated with brain lesions: Clinical phenomenology, cognitive function, and anatomic correlates. *Neurology, 47*(2), 353-361.

Blanes, T., & McGuire, P. (1997). Heterogeneity within obsessive-compulsive disorder: Evidenve for primary and neurodevelopmental subtypes. In M. S. Keshava & R. M. Murray (Eds.), *Neurodevelopmental and Adult Psychopathology* (pp. 206-212). New York, NY: Cambridge University Press.

Boone, K. B., Ananth, J., Philpott, L., Kaur, A., & Djenderedjian, A. (1991). Neuropsychological characteristics of nondepressed adults with obsessive compulsive disorder. *Neuropsychiatry, Neuropsychology and Behavioural Neurology, 4*(2), 96-109.

Bouvard, M., Dirson, S., & Cottraux, J. (1997). Memory processes in obsessive-compulsive washers and obsessive-compulsive cherckes versus a control group. *European Review of Applied Psychology/Revue Europeenne de Psychologie Appliquee, 47*(3), 189-196.

Busatto, G. F., Buchpiguel, C. A., Zamignani, D. R., Garrido, G. E. J., Glabus, M. F., Rosario-Campos, M. C., et al. (2001). Regional cerebral blood flow abnormalities in early-onset obsessive-compulsive disorder: An exploratory SPECT study. *Journal of American Academy of Child and Adolescent Psychiatry, 40*(3), 347-354.

Cavedini, P., Riboldi, G., D'Annucci, A., & Belodi, P. (2002). Decision-making heterogeneity in obsessive-compulsive disorder: Ventromedial prefrontal cortex function predicts different treatment outcomes. *Neuropsychologia, 40*(2), 205-211.

Chamberlain, S. R., Blackwell, A. D., Fineberg, N. A., Robbins, T. W., & Sahakian, B. J. (2005). The neuropsychology of obsessive-compulsive disorder: The importance of failures in cognitive and behavioral inhibition as candidate endophenotypic markers. *Neuroscience and Biobehavioral Reviews, 29*(3), 399-419.

Chamberlain, S. R., Fineberg, N. A., Menzies, L. A., Blackwell, A. D., Bullmore, E. T., Robbins, T. W., et al. (2007). Impaired cognitive flexibility and motor inhibition in unaffected first-degree relatives of patients with obsessive-compulsive disorder. *American Journal of Psychiatry, 164*(2), 335-338.

Christensen, K. J., Kim, S. W., Dysken, M. W., & Hoover, K. M. (1992). Neuropsychological performance in obsessive-compulsive disorder. *Biological Psychiatry, 31*(1), 4-18.

Constans, J. I., Foa, E. B., Franklin, M. E., & Mathews, A. (1995). Memory for actual and imagined events in OC checkers. *Behaviour Research and Therapy, 33*(6), 665-671.

Cottraux, J., & Gerard, D. (1998). Neuroimaging and neuroanatomical issues in obsessive-compulsive disorder: Toward an integrative model--perceived impulsivity. In R. P. Swinson, M. M. Antony, S. Rachman & M. A. Richter (Eds.), *Obsessive-compulsive disorder: Theory, research, and treatment* (pp. 154-180). New York, NY, US: Guilford Press.

Cox, C., Fedio, P., & Rapoport, J. L. (1989). Neuropsychological testing of obsessive-compulsive adolescents. In J. L. Rapoport (Ed.), *Obsessive-compulsive disorder in children and adolescents* (pp. 73-85). Washington, DC: American Psychiatric Press.

Dawkins, K., & Furnham, A. (1989). The colour naming of emotional words. *British Journal of Psychology, 80*, 383-389.

Deckersbach, T., Otto, M. W., Savage, C. R., Baer, L., & Jenike, M. A. (2000). The relationship between semantic organization and memory in obsessive-compulsive disorder. *Psychotherapy and Psychosomatics, 69*(2), 101-107.

Direnfeld, D. M., Pato, M. T., & Roberts, J. E. (2001). *Attentional biases in obsessive compulsive disorder: relationship to symptomatology and treatment.* Paper presented at the 2001 Meeting of the Association for the Advancement of Behavior Therapy.

Dirson, S., Bouvard, M., Cottraux, J., & Martin, R. (1995). Visual memory impairment in patients with obsessive-compulsive disorder: A controlled study. *Psychotherapy and Psychosomatics, 63*(1), 22-31.

Enright, S. J., Beech, A. R., & Claridge, G. S. (1995). A further investigation of cognitive inhibition in obsessive-compulsive disorder and other anxiety disorders. *Personality and Individual Differences, 19*(4), 535-542.

Foa, E. B., Ilai, D., McCarthy, P. R., Shoyer, B., & Murdock, T. (1993). Information processing in obsessive-compulsive disorder. *Cognitive Therapy and Research, 17*(2), 173-189.

Franke, P., Maier, W., Hardt, J., Frieboes, R., Lichtermann, D., & Hain, C. (1993). Assessment of frontal lobe functioning in schizophrenia and unipolar major depression. *Psychopathology, 26*(2), 76-84.

Frost, R. O., & Gross, R. C. (1993). The hoarding of possessions. *Behaviour Research and Therapy, 31*(4), 367-381.

Gambini, O., Abbruzzese, M., & Scarone, S. (1993). Smooth pursuit and saccadic eye movements and Wisconsin Card Sorting Test perfomance in obsessive-compulsive disorder. *Psychiatry Research, 48*(3), 191-200.

Gershuny, B. S., & Sher, K. J. (1995). Compulsive checking and anxiety in a nonclinical sample: Differences in cognition, behavior, personality, and affect. *Journal of Psychopathology and Behavioral Assessment, 17*(1), 19-38.

Greisberg, S., & McKay, D. (2003). Neuropsychology of obsessive-compulsive disorder: A review and treatment implications. *Clinical Psychology Review, 23*(1), 95-117.

Grisham, J. R., Brown, T. A., Liverant, G. I., & Campbell-Sills, L. (2005). The distinctiveness of compulsive hoarding from obsessive-compulsive disorder. *Journal of Anxiety Disorders, 19*(7), 767-779.

Head, D., Bolton, D., & Hymas, N. (1989). Deficit in cognitive shifting ability in patients with obsessive-compulsive disorder. *Biological Psychiatry, 25*(7), 929-937.

Hermans, D., Martens, K., De Cort, K., Pieters, G., & Eelen, P. (2003). Reality monitoring and metacognitive beliefs related to cognitive confidence in obsessive-compulsive disorder. *Behaviour Research and Therapy, 41*(4), 383-401.

Hoenig, K., Hochrein, A., Muller, D. J., & Wagner, M. (2002). Different negative priming impairments in schizophrenia and subgroups of obsessive-compulsive disorder. *Psychological Medicine, 32*(3), 459-468.

Hollander, E., Schiffman, E., Cohen, B., Rivera-Stein, M. A., Rosen, W., Gorman, J. M., et al. (1990). Signs of central nervous system dysfunction in obsessive-compulsive disorder. *Archives of General Psychiatry, 47*(1), 27-32.

Hymas, N., Lees, A., Bolton, D., Epps, K., & Head, D. (1991). The neurology of obsessional slowness. *Brain, 114*(5), 2203-2233.

Insel, T. R. (1992). Toward a neuroanatomy of obsessive-compulsive disorder. *Archives of General Psychiatry, 49*(9), 739-744.

Jenike, M. A., & Brotman, A. W. (1984). The EEG in obsessive-compulsive disorder. *Journal of Clinical Psychiatry, 45*(3), 122-124.

Kim, M. S., Park, P. J., Shin, M. S., & Kwon, J. S. (2002). Neuropsychological profile in patients with obsessive-compulsive disorder over a period of 4-month treatment. *Journal of Psychiatric Research, 36*(4), 257-265.

Kuelz, A. K., Hohagen, F., & Voderholzer, U. (2004). Neuropsychological performance in obsessive-compulsive disorder: A critical review. *Biological Psychiatry, 65*(3), 185-236.

Kuelz, A. K., Riemann, D., Halsband, U., Vielhaber, K., Unterrainer, J., Kordon, A., et al. (2006). Neuropsychological impairment in obsessive-compulsive disorder-improvement over the course of cognitive behavioral treatment. *Journal of Clinical and Experimental Neuropsychology, 28*(8), 1273-1287.

Kwon, J. S., Kim, J. J., Lee, D. W., Lee, J. S., Lee, D. S., Kim, M. S., et al. (2003). Neural correlates of clinical symptoms and cognitive dysfunctions in obsessive-compulsive disorder. *Psychiatry Research: Neuroimaging, 122*(1), 37-47.

Kyrios, M., Wainwright, K., Purcell, R., Pantelis, C., & Maruff, P. (1999). *Neuropsychological performance in subtypes of obsessive-compulsive disorder.* Paper presented at the 33rd conference of the Association for Advancement of Behavior Therapy, Toronto, ON.

Lavy, E. H., van Oppen, P., & van den Hout, M. A. (1994). Selective processing of emotional information in obsessive-compulsive disorder. *Behaviour Research and Therapy, 32*(2), 243-246.

Lawrence, N. S., Wooderson, S., Mataix-Cols, D., David, R., Speckens, A., & Phillips, M. L. (2006). Decision making and set shifting impairments are associated with distinct symptom dimensions in obsessive-compulsive disorder. *Neuropsychology, 20*(4), 409-419.

Lezak, M. (1995). *Neuropsychological assessment.* New York, NY: Oxford University Press.

Logan, G. D., Cowan, W. B., & Davis, K. A. (1984). On the ability to inhibit simple and choice reaction time response: A model and a method. *Journal of Experimental Psychology: Human Perception and Performance, 10*(2), 276-291.

MacDonald, P. A., Antony, M. M., MacLeod, C. M., & Richter, M. A. (1997). Memory and confidence in memory judgments among individuals with obsessive-compulsive disorder and non-clinical controls. *Behaviour Research and Therapy, 35*(6), 497-505.

MacLeod, C. M. (1996). Anxiety and cognitive processes. In I. G. Sarason, G. R. Pierce & B. R. Sarason (Eds.), *Cognitive interference: Theories, methods, and findings* (pp. 47-76). Hillsdale, NJ: Lawrence Erlbaum.

MacLeod, C. M., & Mathews, A. (1988). Anxiety and the allocation of attention to threat. *Quarterly Journal of Experimental Psychology Section A: Human Experimental Psychology, 40*(4-A), 653-670.

MacLeod, C. M., Mathews, A., & Tata, P. (1986). Attentional bias in emotional disorders. *Journal of Abnormal Psychology, 95*(1), 15-20.

Malloy, P. (1987). Frontal lobe dysfunction in obsessive-compulsive disorder. In E. Perecman (Ed.), *The frontal lobes revisited.* New York, NY: The IRBN Press.

Martin, A., Wiggs, C. L., Altemus, M., Rubenstein, C., & Murphy, D. L. (1995). Working memory as assessed by subject-ordered tasks in patients with obsessive-compulsive disorder. *Journal of Clinical and Experimental Neuropsychology, 17*(5), 786-792.

Martin, D. J., Oren, Z., & Boone, K. B. (1991). Major depressives' and dysthymics' performance on the Wisconsin Card Sorting Test. *Journal of Clinical Psychology, 47*(5), 684-690.

Martin, V., Huber, M., Rief, W., & Exner, C. (2008). Comparative cognitive profiles of obsessive-compulsive disorder and schizophrenia. *Archives of Clinical Neuropsychology, 23*, 487-500.

Martinot, J. L., Allilaire, J. F., Mazoyer, B. M., Hantouche, E., Huret, J. D., Legaut-Demare, F., et al. (1990). Obsessive-compulsive disorder: A clinical, neuropsychological and positron emission tomography study. *Acta Psychiatrica Scandinavica, 82*(3), 233-242.

Mataix-Cols, D., Junque, C., Sanchez-Turet, M., Vallejo, J., Verger, K., & Barrios, M. (1999). Neuropsychological functioning in a subclinical obsessive-compulsive sample. *Biological Psychiatry, 45*(7), 898-904.

Mataix-Cols, D., Marks, I. M., Greist, J. H., Kobak, K. A., & Baer, L. (2002). Obsessive-compulsive symptom dimensions as predictors of compliance with and response to behaviour therapy: Results from a controlled trial. *Psychotherapy and Psychosomatics, 71*, 255-262.

Mataix-Cols, D., Wooderson, S., Lawrence, N. S., Brammer, M. J., Speckens, A., & Phillips, M. L. (2004). Neural correlates of washing, checking, and hoarding symptom dimensions in obsessive-compulsive disorder. *Archives of General Psychiatry, 61*(6), 564-576.

McKay, D., Abramowitz, J. S., Calamari, J. E., Kyrios, M., Radomsky, A. S., Sookman, D., et al. (2004). A critical evaluation of obsessive-compulsive disorder subtypes: Symptoms versus mechanisms. *Clinical Psychology Review, 24*, 283-313.

McNally, R. J., & Kohlbeck, P. A. (1993). Reality monitoring in obsessive-compulsive disorder. *Behaviour Research and Therapy, 31*(3), 249-253.

Milliery, M., Bouvard, M., Aupetit, J., & Cottraux, J. (2000). Sustained attention in patients with obsessive-compulsive disorder: A controlled study. *Psychiatry Research, 96*(3), 199-209.

Mindus, P., Rasmussen, S. A., & Lindquist, C. (1994). Neurosurgical treatment for refractory obsessive-compulsive disorder: Implications for understanding frontal lobe function. *Journal of Neuropsychiatry and Clinical Neurosciences, 6*(4), 467-477.

Mogg, K., Mathews, A., & Eysenck, M. (1992). Attentional bias to threat in clinical anxiety states. *Cognition and Emotion, 6*(2), 149-159.

Mogg, K., Millar, N., & Bradley, B. P. (2000). Biases in eye movements to threatening facial expression in generalized anxiety disorder and depressive disorder. *Journal of Abnormal Psychology, 109*(4), 695-704.

Moritz, S., Birkner, C., Kloss, M., Jacobsen, D., Fricke, S., Bothern, A., et al. (2001). Impact of comorbid depressive symptoms on neuropsychological performance in obsessive-compulsive disorder. *Journal of Abnormal Psychology, 110*(4), 653-657.

Moritz, S., Birkner, C., Kloss, M., Jahn, H., Hand, I., Haasen, C., et al. (2002). Executive functioning in obsessive-compulsive disorder, unipolar depression, and schizophrenia. *Archives of Clinical Neuropsychology, 17*(5), 477-483.

Moritz, S., Heeren, D., Andresen, B., & Krausz, M. (2001). An analysis of the specificity and the syndromal correlates of verbal memory impairments in schizophrenia. *Psychiatry Research, 101*(1), 23-31.

Moritz, S., Kloss, M., Jacobsen, D., Kellner, M., Andresen, B., Fricke, S., et al. (2005). Extent, profile and specificity of visuospatial impairment in obsessive-compulsive disorder (OCD). *Journal of Clinical and Experimental Neuropsychology, 27*(7), 795-814.

Moritz, S., Kloss, M., Katenkamp, B., Birkner, C., & Hand, I. (1999). Neurocognitive functioning in OCD before and after treatment. *CNS Spectrum, 4*, 21-22.

Muller, J., & Roberts, J. E. (2005). Memory and attention in obsessive-compulsive disorder: A review. *Journal of Anxiety Disorders, 19*(1), 1-28.

Muller, S. V., Johannes, S., Wieringa, B., Weber, A., Muller-Vahl, K., Matzke, M., et al. (2003). Disturbed monitoring and response inhibition in patients with Gilles de la Tourette Syndrome and co-morbid obsessive compulsive disorder. *Behavioural Neurology, 14*(1), 29-37.

Nakao, T., Nakagawa, A., Nakatani, E., Nabeyama, M., Sanematsu, H., Yoshiura, T., et al. (2009). Working memory dysfunction in obsessive-compulsive disorder: A neuropsychological and functional MRI study. *Journal of Psychiatric Research, 43*, 784-791.

Nielen, M. M. A., & Den Boer, J. A. (2003). Neuropsychological performances of OCD patients before and after treatment with fluoxetine: Evidence fo persistent cognitive deficits. *Psychological Medicine, 33*(5), 917-925.

Omori, I. M., Murata, Y., Yamanishi, T., Nakaaki, S., Akechi, T., Mikuni, M., et al. (2007). The differential impact of executive attention dysfunction on episodic memory in obsessive-compulsive disorder with checking symptoms vs. those with washing symptoms. *Journal of Psychiatric Research, 41*(9), 776-784.

Osterrieth, P. (1944). Le test du copie d'une figure complex: Contribution a l'etude de la perception et de la memoire. *Archives de Psychologie, 30*, 286-350.

Penades, R., Catalan, R., Rubia, K., Andres, S., Salamero, M., & Gasto, C. (2007). Impaired response inhibition in obsessive-compulsive disorder. *European Psychiatry, 22*(6), 404-410.

Purcell, R., Maruff, P., Kyrios, M., & Pantelis, C. (1998a). Cognitive deficits in obsessive-compulsive disorder on tests of frontal-striatal function. *Biological Psychiatry, 43*(5), 348-357.

Purcell, R., Maruff, P., Kyrios, M., & Pantelis, C. (1998b). Neuropsychological deficits in obsessive-compulsive disorder: A comparison with unipolar depression, panic disorder, and normal controls. *Archives of General Psychiatry, 55*(5), 415-423.

Radomsky, A. S., & Rachman, S. (1999). Memory bias in obsessive-compulsive disoder (OCD). *Behaviour Research and Therapy, 37*(7), 605-618.

Radomsky, A. S., Rachman, S., & Hammond, D. (2001). Memory bias, confidence and responsability in compulsive checking. *Behaviour Research and Therapy, 39*(7), 813-822.

Rapoport, J. L., & Wise, S. P. (1988). Obsessive-compulsive disorder: Evidence for basal ganglia dysfunction. *Psychopharmacology Bulletin, 24*(3), 380-384.

Rasmussen, S. A., & Eisen, J. L. (1991). Phenomenology of OCD: Clinical subtypes, heterogeneity, and coexistence. In J. Zohar, T. Insel & S. A. Rasmussen (Eds.), *The psychobiology of obsessive-compulsive disorder* (pp. 13-43). New York, NY: Springer.

Robinson, D., Wu, H., Munne, R. A., Ashtari, M., Alvir, J., Lerner, G., et al. (1995). Reduced caudate nucleus volume in obsessive-compulsive disorder. *Archives of General Psychiatry, 52*(5), 393-398.

Rosenberg, D. R., & Keshavan, M. S. (1998). Toward a neurodevelopmental model of obsessive-compulsive disorder. *Biological Psychiatry, 43*(9), 623-640.

Rosenberg, D. R., Averbach, D. H., O'Hearn, K. M., Seymour, A. B., Birmaher, B., & Sweeney, J. A. (1997). Oculomotor response in inhibition abnormalities in pediatric obsessive-compulsive disorder. *Archives of General Psychiatry, 54*(9), 831-838.

Rosenberg, D. R., Dick, E. L., O'Hearn, K. M., & Sweeney, J. A. (1997). Response-inhibition deficits in obsessive-compulsive disorder: An indicator of dysfunction in frontostriatal circuits. *Journal of Psychiatry and Neuroscience, 22*(1), 29-38.

Roth, R. M., Milovan, D. L., Baribeau, J., O'Connor, K., & Todorov, C. (2004). Organizational strategy use in obsessive-compulsive disorder. *Psychiatry Research, 128*(3), 267-272.

Roth, R. M., Milovan, D., Baribeau, J., & O'Connor, K. (2005). Neuropsychological functioning in early- and late-onset obsessive-compulsive disorder. *Journal of Neuropsychiatry and Clinical Neurosciences, 17*(2), 208-213.

Rubenstein, C. S., Peynircioglu, Z. F., Chambless, D. L., & Pigott, T. A. (1993). Memory in sub-clinical obsessive-compulsive checkers. *Behaviour Research and Therapy, 31*(8), 759-765.

Savage, C. R., & Rauch, S. L. (2000). Cognitive deficits in obsessive-compulsive disorder. *American Journal of Psychiatry, 157*(7), 1182-1183.

Savage, C. R., Baer, L., Keuthen, N. J., Brown, H. D., Rauch, S. L., & Jenike, M. A. (1999). Organizational strategies mediate nonverbal memory impairment in obsessive-compulsive disorder. *Biological Psychiatry, 45*(7), 905-916.

Savage, C. R., Keuthen, N. J., Jenike, M. A., Brown, H. D., Baer, L., Kendrick, A. D., et al. (1996). Recall and recognition memory in obsessive-compulsive disorder. *Journal of Neuropsychiatry and Clinical Neurosciences, 8*(1), 99-103.

Saxena, S., Brody, A. L., Maidment, K. M., Dunkin, J. J., Colgan, M., Alborizan, S., et al. (1999). Localized orbifrontal and subcortical metabolic changes and predictors of response to paroxetine treatment in obsessive-compulsive disorder. *Neuropsychopharmacology, 21*(6), 683-693.

Saxena, S., Brody, A. L., Schwartz, J. M., & Baxter, L. R. (1998). Neuroimaging and frontal-subcortical circuitry in obsessive-compulsive disorder. *British Journal of Psychiatry, 173*(Suppl 35), 26-37.

Schmidtke, K., Schorb, A., Winkelmann, G., & Hohagen, F. (1998). Cognitive frontal lobe dysfunction in obsessive-compulsive disorder. *Biological Psychiatry, 43*(9), 666-673.

Sher, K. J., Frost, R. O., & Otto, R. (1983). Cognitive deficits in compulsive checkers: An exploratory study. *Behaviour Research and Therapy, 21*(4), 357-363.

Sher, K. J., Frost, R. O., Kushner, M., Crews, T. M., & Alexander, J. E. (1989). Memory deficits in compulsive checkers: Replication and extension in a clinical sample. *Behaviour Research and Therapy, 27*(1), 65-69.

Sher, K. J., Mann, B., & Frost, R. O. (1984). Cognitive dysfunction in compulsive checkers: Further explorations. *Behaviour Research and Therapy, 22*(5), 493-502.

Shin, M. S., Park, P. J., Kim, M. S., Lee, Y. H., Ha, T. H., & Kwon, J. S. (2004). Deficits of organizational strategy and visual memory in obsessive-compulsive disorder. *Neuropsychology, 18*(4), 665-672.

Simpson, H. B., Rosen, W., Huppert, J. D., Lin, S., H., Foa, E. B., & Liebowitz, M. R. (2006). Are ther reliable neuropsychological deficits in obsessive-compulsive disorder? *Journal of Psychiatric Research, 40*(3), 247-257.

Stein, D. J. (2002). Obsessive-compulsive disorder. *The Lancet, 360*(9330), 397-405.

Steketee, G., & Frost, R. O. (2003). Compulsive hoarding: Current status of the research. *Clinical Psychology Review, 23*(7), 905-927.

Szeszko, P. R., Robinson, D., Alvir, J. M., Bilder, R. M., Lencz, T., Ashtari, M., et al. (1999). Orbital frontal and amygdala volume reductions in obsessive-compulsive disorder. *Archives of General Psychiatry, 56*(10), 913-919.

Tallis, F., Pratt, P., & Jamani, N. (1999). Obsessive compulsive disorder, checking, and non-verbal memory: A neuropsychological investigation. *Behaviour Research and Therapy, 37*(2), 161-166.

Tata, P. R., Leibowitz, J. A., Prunty, M. J., Cameron, M., & Pickering, A. D. (1996). Attentional bias in Obsessional Compulsive Disorder. *Behaviour Research and Therapy, 34*(1), 53-60.

Tolin, D. F., Abramowitz, J. S., Brigidi, B. D., Amir, N., Street, G. P., & Foa, E. B. (2001). Memory and memory confidence in obsessive-compulsive disorder. *Behaviour Research and Therapy, 39*(8), 913-927.

Tonkonogy, J. M., Smith, T. W., & Barreira, P. J. (1994). Obsessive-compulsive disorders in Pick's disease. *Journal of Neuropsychiatry and Clinical Neurosciences, 6*(2), 176-180.

van der Wee, N. J., Ramsey, N. F., Jansma, J. M., Denys, D. A., van Megen, H. J., Westenberg, H. M., et al. (2003). Spatial working memory deficits in obsessive-compulsive disorder are associated with excessive engagement of the medial frontal cortex *Neuroimage, 20*(4), 2271-2280.

Veale, D. M., Sahakian, B. J., Owen, A. M., & Marks, I. M. (1996). Specific cognitive deficits in tests sensitive to frontal lobe dysfunction in obsessive-compulsive disorder. *Psychological Medicine, 26*(6), 1261-1269.

Watkins, L. H., Sahakian, B. J., Robertson, M. M., Veale, D. M., Rogers, R. D., Pickard, K. M., et al. (2005). Executive function in Tourette's syndrome and obsessive-compulsive disorder. *Psychological Medicine, 35*(4), 571-582.

Wechsler, D. (1987). *Wechsler Memory Scale-Revised.* San Antonio, TX: The Psychological Corporation.

Wincze, J. P. (2001). The role of under-inclusion in the etiology of compulsive hoarding behavior. *Dissertation Abstracts International: Section B: The Sciences and Engineering, 62*(2-B), 1062.

Woods, C. M., Vevea, J. L., Chambless, D. L., & Bayen, U. J. (2002). Are compulsive checkers impaired in memory? A meta-analytic review. *Clinical Psychology: Science and Practice, 9*(4), 353-366.

Zielinski, C. M., Taylor, M. A., & Juzwin, K. R. (1991). Neuropsychological deficits in obsessive-compulsive disorder. *Neuropsychiatry, Neuropsychology and Behavioural Neurology, 4*(2), 110-126.

Zitterl, W., Urban, C., Linzmayer, L., Aigner, M., Demal, U., Semler, B., et al. (2001). Memory deficits in patients with DSM-IV obsessive-compulsive disorder. *Psychopathology, 34*(3), 113-117.

Chapter 3

FUNCTIONAL NEUROIMAGING STUDIES

ABSTRACT

In this chapter, recent research examining functional neuroimaging studies was examined. Most data come from positron emission tomography (PET), functional magnetic resonance imaging (fMRI) and single photon emission tomography (SPECT) studies. Different study paradigms were considered such as: 1) comparing individuals in baseline states; 2) scanning patients during symptom provocation; 3) scanning patients during performance of a cognitive task; 4) scanning patients before and after treatment. Regardless the type of paradigm being considered, several differences were found between OCD patients and controls individuals. No doubt that functional neuroimaging studies are giving an interesting contribute to the understanding of a complex condition such as OCD.

INTRODUCTION

Advances in neuroimaging techniques have led to a better understanding of brain-behavior relationships in OCD. Most data come from positron emission tomography (PET), functional magnetic resonance imaging (fMRI) and single photon emission tomography (SPECT) studies. These non invasive brain imaging techniques permit unprecedented in vivo "biopsies" of brain structure, chemistry, and function. Besides different techniques, four basic research design have been used to investigate the pathophysiology of OCD: (a) comparing OCD patients with healthy controls in neutral or baseline states, (b) scanning OCD patients during symptom provocation and in control comparison states, (c) scanning OCD patients during performance of a cognitive task and comparison conditions, and (d) scanning OCD patients before and after treatment to measure cerebral activity changes.

3.1. Comparing OCD Patients with Healthy Controls in Neutral or Baseline States

McGuire et al. (1994) and Lucey et al. (1995) identified a negative correlation between an obsessive-compulsive symptom dimension and right parietal Cerebral Blood Flow (rCBF) through PET studies. Additionally, single photon emission tomography (SPECT) studies measuring rCBF indicate parietal abnormalities in OCD (Rubin, Villanueva-Meyer, Ananth, Trajmar & Mena, 1992; Lucey et al., 1995).

Lucey et al. (1997) utilised SPECT and identified reduced caudate regional rCBF in OCD at rest, not only when compared to healthy controls, but also when compared to controls with panic disorder. Edmonstone et al. (1994) also using SPECT, found evidence for abnormal basal ganglia metabolism in OCD that was absent in a group of clinically depressed controls matched for medication.

Lacerda et al. (2003) used SPECT to examine brain-activation patterns of 16 patients with OCD versus 17 control subjects at rest. The region of interest method (ROI) was used. OCD patients showed a significantly higher rCBF in four regions: the right superior and inferior frontal cortex and the right and left thalamus. Others functional brain-imaging studies consistently report increased rCBF or metabolic activity in frontal areas and brain regions that compose the frontal–subcortical circuits in OCD patients (Alptekin et al., 2001; Baxter et al., 1988; Hoehn-Saric, Pearlson, Harris, Machlin & Camargo, 1991; McGuire et al., 1994; Rauch et al., 1994; Rubin et al., 1992; Swedo, Rapoport, Leonard, Lenane & Cheslow, 1989; Machlin et al., 1991; Rubin, Ananth, Villanueva-Meyer, Trajmar & Mena 1995). Moreover, Lacerda et al. (2003) highlighted that illness duration positively correlated with rCBF the superior portion of the frontal lobes (bilaterally) and in the right thalamus.

Maihofner et al. (2007), using MEG (magnetoencephalographic), compared individuals with OCD to a healthy control group (n=10 per group). MEG is an additional neuroimaging method that combines both high temporal and spatial resolution and it is a potentially powerful tool for determining localization of brain function. The authors found evidence for an increase of fast MEG activity over the left hemisphere in the OCD group. Moreover, they demonstrated that OCD patients show abnormally fast MEG activity over their left superior temporal gyrus (STG) and an enrichment of slow MEG activity over the left dorsal-lateral-prefrontal-cortex (DLPFC). These findings complemented previous studies which have suggested a dysfunction of frontal cortices (e.g. OF and DLPFC), anterior cingulate cortex (ACC), basal ganglia, and other subcortical and limbic structures as neural basis for the pathogenesis in OCD (Saxena & Rauch, 2000; Rauch et al., 2001). The involvement of temporal regional in the pathogenesis of OCD is suggested by PET and SPECT studies (Cottraux et al., 1996; Hendler et al., 1999; Lucey et al., 1995; Simpson & Baldwin, 1995), morphometric magnetic resonance study in OCD patients (Choi et al., 2006), and investigation of brain activation during symptom provocation in OCD study (Adler et al., 2000).

The enrichment of slow MEG activity in the left DLPFC is in line with with results of EEG investigation which has demonstrated a frontal-temporal dysfunction with a significant increase of frontal slow wave activity compared to healthy subjects (Tot, Ozge, Comelekoglu, Yazici & Bal, 2002; Karadag et al., 2003). Moreover, activation of the DLPFC has been consistently showed during symptom provocation in OCD (Adler et al., 2000; Nakao et al., 2005a).

Szeszko et al. (2005) investigated white matter abnormalities in individuals with OCD and healthy volunteers (n=15 per group). They used diffusion tensor imaging (DTI) (an in vivo MRI technique) to test abnormalities in anterior cingulate white matter microstructure and white matter integrity across the entire brain. Patients with OCD showed abnormal white matter microstructure within the anterior cingulate gyrus. The involvement of anterior cingulate in OCD is consistent with findings of previous studies which highlighted the relevance of such region in monitoring and resolving conflict during information processing, in fear conditioning and reward expectancy, and in tasks of response inhibition (Braver, Barch, Gray, Molfese & Snyder, 2001; Frankland, Bontempi, Talton, Kaczmarek & Silva, 2004; Shidara & Richmond, 2002; Schmidtke et al., 1998). Moreover, microstructural alteration may reflect a defect in connectivity which could to contribute to pathogenesis of disorder (Rosenberg et al., 1997; Szeszko et al., 2005). From the examination of the rest of the brain white matter, the authors identified abnormalities in several additional areas: the posterior cingulate gyrus, bilateral supramarginal gyri within the parietal lobes, and the left lingual gyrus within the occipital lobe.

Szeszko et al. (2008) used a voxel-based morphometry to examine a grey matter structures alterations in in 37 psychotropic drug-naive pediatric patients with OCD vs 26 control subjects. Individuals with OCD had significantly more grey matter in the right and left putamen and OFC compared to healthy volunteers. There was a positive association between symptoms severity and more left putamen/right OFC grey matter. The results of study indicated that the putamen was involved in pathophysiology of OCD. Such brain region has been hypothesized to play an important role in motor and cognitive control, which has particular relevance for neurobiological models of OCD (Szeszko et al., 2008). In fact, other studies evidenced: (1) an increase in grey matter volume bilaterally in the putamen in adults with OCD compared to healthy volunteers (Pujol et al., 2004) and (2) hypermetabolism in the putamen among patients with OCD (Perani et al., 1995).

Moreover, Szezko et al. (2008) highlighted more pronounced abnormalities in lateral as opposed to medial OF regions among patients with OCD compared to healthy volunteers. The lateral portion of OFC plays a role in the interruption of behaviors based on prior reward values of stimulus-response associations (Elliot, Dolan & Frith, 2000) and may thus have relevance for OCD patients' difficulty discontinuing their compulsions. Szeszko and coll. also observed more grey matter in patients compared to healthy volunteers in several other brain regions including the frontal pole, STG, and parietal lobe. In addition, several areas of less gray matter in the occipital cortex were observed in OCD patients in both the right and left hemispheres.

Gilbert et al. (2008) measured gray matter volume in 25 adult OCD patients and 20 adult healthy controls using voxel-based morphometry (VBM). The results showed a significant gray matter volumetric differences in OCD patients relative to controls in several prefrontale regions (bilateral BA9, BA6, BA46 and right BA8) (controls>patients) and bilateral midbrain (patients>controls). Stepwise regression analyses revealed highly significant relationships between greater total OCD symptom severity and smaller gray matter volumes in dorsal cortical regions and larger gray matter volumes in bilateral midbrain. Despite such findings are inconclusive regarding the neural substrates for OCD, they highlighted specific patterns of gray matter volume abnormalities in prefrontal cortex and midbrain in OCD patients, which are primarily associated with the global severity of the disorder.

3.2. Scanning OCD Patients During Symptom Provocation

In a recent meta-analysis, Rotge et al. (2008) used the activation likelihood estimation method to evidence the neural substrates of OCD during symptom-provocation task. This study confirmed the importance of cortico–striato–thalamo–cortical circuit that have been shown to be overactive in OCD. Besides the involvement both the ACC and OFC, Rotge et al. (2008) highlighted the involvement of other cerebral structures in the performance of a symptom provocation task: the right anterior PFC, the left DLPFC, the left precuneus, the right premotor cortex, the left STG, the bilateral external globus pallidus, the right thalamus, the left hippocampus and the right uncus. These results showed activation in unexpected regions of the brain, such as the temporal and parietal cortices and confirmed the importance of cortico–striato–thalamo–cortical circuits that have been shown to be overactive in OCD. Moreover, the authors suggested that these regions share a critical function in the genesis or mediation of OC symptoms (Rotge et al., 2008).

Nakao et al. (2005b) used fMRI to observe the brain activation of 10 OCD patients during neuropsychological task (Stroop task) and symptom provocation task (imagination of words-related to their symptoms) before and after symptom improvement. Each patient was randomly assigned to receive either phamarcotherapy (fluvoxamine) or behaviour therapy for 12 weeks. A voxel-based approach in Statistical Parametric Mapping analysis was used. The authors found that before treatment, patients showed brain activation in the left prefrontal (DLPFC) and parietal cortices and right cerebellum during the Stroop task. There were similar brain activations in normal control subjects during such neuropsychological task (Nakao et al, 2005a). In contrast to previous studies, however, Nakao et al. (2005b) were unable to identify ACC activation during the Stroop task in patients before treatment. The absence of baseline period may have accounted for such different findings. After treatment, patients generally showed increased activation in bilateral DLPFC, bilateral ACC, parietal cortices, and cerebellum. Such areas may play a role in coordinating complex mental and non motor higher functions (Andreasen, Paradiso & O'Leary, 1998; Schmahmann and Pandya 1997). Increased activation after treatment, evidenced that OC symptoms might suppress these areas and could negative impact cognitive performance in OCD (Nakao et al., 2005b). Regard the provocation task, before treatment, patients showed activation in the left OFC, temporal cortex, and parietal cortex. After treatment, patients showed decreased activation in the OFC, ACC, putamen, insula, temporal cortex, occipital cortex, and cerebellum.

In a comparative symptom-provocation study to examine the neural correlates of different symptom dimensions of OCD, Mataix-Cols et al., (2004) found that washing, checking, and hoarding symptom dimensions of OCD were mediated by distinct but partially overlapping neural systems. Specifically, patients demonstrated significantly greater activation than controls in bilateral ventromedial prefrontal regions and right caudate nucleus (washing); putamen/globus pallidus, thalamus, and dorsal cortical areas (checking); left precentral gyrus and right orbitofrontal cortex (hoarding); and left occipitotemporal regions (aversive, symptom-unrelated) (Mataix-Cols et al., 2004).

3.3. Scanning OCD Patients During Performance Cognitive Tasks

In an event-related potential study, twenty drug-free OCD patients showed an enhanced auditory P600 , measured during the anticipatory period of working memory test (a computerized version of the Wechsler digit span test) at the right temporal-parietal area and prolonged latencies at the right parietal region when compared with healthy controls (Papageorgiou & Rabavilas, 2003). Furthermore, OCD patients showed a significantly impaired memory performance.

Nakao et al. (2005a), using fMRI, directly examined the relationship between brain and neuropsychological dysfunctions in 24 OCD patients compared with 14 normal controls. They used a voxel-based approach and administered a large neuropsychological test battery (WAIS-R, Stroop test, WSCT, WMS-R and R-OCFT). They found no significant between-group differences and no evidence of neuropsychological deficits in the sample of patients with OCD. Nakao et al. (2005a) found that the patients showed weaker activation than the normal controls in the ACC and the right caudate nucleus. According to the authors, the absence of baseline and control periods may explain the paradoxical activation of the ACC and the caudate nucleus in OCD during the task condition of the Stroop test. It was possible that that the function of those areas of the OCD patients had already been activated during the control condition or at rest.

Different patterns of brain over- and underactivation have been found in a symptom provocation study where the OCD patients were required to exert response inhibition (Roth et al., 2007). Using fMRI and a go/no-go task, Roth et al. (2007) examined the neural substrates of such cognitive function in 12 adults with OCD and 14 healthy comparison subjects. The role for cortico-striato-thalamic circuitry abnormality in dysfunctional inhibitory control in OCD was confirmed but there were no significant performance differences between groups on go/no-go task. Regard the different brain activations, healthy adults showed predominantly right-hemisphere activation including the right inferior frontal gyrus, whereas the patient group showed a more diffuse, bilateral pattern of activation. Furthermore, the OCD group demonstrated less activation than the comparison group in several right-hemisphere regions during response inhibition, including right thalamus, inferior and medial frontal gyri. The authors reported negative correlations between OCD symptom severity and activations of the right OFC and dorsal anterior cingulate gyrus during response inhibition. They speculated that greater ability to activate these regions contributes to a better ability to suppress unwanted thoughts and behaviors in patients with OCD. Moreover, the study evidenced that OCD severity was positively correlated with activation of the left thalamus, suggesting that the thalamus and associated neural circuitry may play a role in symptom generation or intensity. It is possible that overactivation of frontal subregions observed in resting and symptom-provocation in most of previous studies may reflect attempts to inhibit the expression or intensity of symptoms driven by overactivation in other regions such as the thalamus.

Yucel et al. (2007) investigated the functional and biochemical properties of the media frontal cortex (MFC). They used volume localized proton magnetic resonance spectroscopy and fMRI to examine MFC during a task encompassing inhibitory control processes (the Multi-Source Interference Task), in 19 patients with OCD and 19 control subjects. As in previous studies (Pujol et al., 2004; Saxena & Rauch, 2000; Rauch, Shin & Wright, 2003) the authors found abnormal high MFC activity.

This pattern of activation, which is commonly seen in fMRI studies of OCD patients, may reflect a compensatory response to a primary neuronal abnormality in such region (van Den Heuvel et al., 2005; Pujol et al, 1999). Some researchers argued that the MFC may be involved in reduced capacity of patients with OCD to inhibit intrusive or ritualistic cognitions and motor response tendencies (Chamberlain et al., 2005; van Den Heuvel et al., 2005; Modell, Mountz, Curtis & Greden, 1989).

3.4. Studies before and after Treatment

Psychological interventions, such as CBT, are able to modify activity in dysfunctional neural circuitries linked to development of OCD (Roffman, Marci, Glick, Dougherty & Rauch, 2005). The change in patients' symptoms and maladaptive behaviour at the mind level with psychological techniques could potentially normalize the brain at the functional level in the same way as faulty brain signals resulting from dysfunctional neural circuitries lead to psychopathological behaviour (Kumari, 2006).

The first neuroimaging studies of psychotherapy, including OCD patients, were conducted by Baxter and colleagues (Baxter et al. 1992). These authors used PET to investigate resting cerebral glucose metabolism in patients with OCD. Patients received 10 weeks of either fluoxetine (n=9) or behaviour therapy (BT) (n=9), the latter focused on exposure and response prevention. Despite some limitations (medication and psychotherapy treatment groups were combined, presence of psychiatric comorbidities), the authors found significant change in brain function following psychotherapy treatment. Importantly, the change occurred in the regions consistent with the known pathophysiology of OCD (right caudate nucleus, OFC, and thalamus). Further, among patients who responded favourably to treatment, Baxter et al. (1992) observed an uncoupling of hyperactivity in the right caudate, OFC, and thalamus.

Schwartz, Stoessel, Baxter, Martin and Phelps (1996) examined nine patients with OCD and without active psychiatric comorbidities. Response to BT was associated with reduction of metabolic activity in the caudate nucleus, especially on the right side. Moreover, specifically in patients who responded to psychotherapy, the cortico-striato-thalamic abnormality disappeared with treatment. Also, Nakatani et al., (2003), using xenon-enhanced computed tomography (Xe-CT), reported a significant reduction in the right caudate following BT in a large sample (n=62) of OCD patients. The reported treatment studies yielded comparable results: (1) BT reduced metabolism in the caudate nucleus, and (2) both fluoxetine and psychotherapy for OCD appeared to uncouple dysfunctional cortico-striato-thalamic circuitry.

Brody et al. (1998) demonstrated that patients with OCD responded in a different way to behavioral therapy and to pharmacotherapy with fluoxetine. Among patients who received BT, they observed a positive correlation between treatment response and baseline metabolism in the left OFC and they proposed that patients with increased OFC activity at baseline may be predisposed to benefit from extinction-based therapy for OCD. This finding is consistent with Roth et al. (2007) study in which they observed negative correlations between OCD symptom severity and activations of the OFC.

Matsumoto et al. (2008), using SPECT, provided evidence that OFC is involved in the pathophysiology of OCD. In a case report study with OCD patient and healthy control individual, they have investigated changes following more than one episode of relapse. Despite OC symptoms were different during two relapse episode, the authors found a recurrent hyperperfusion in the right anterior lateral OFC. Matsumoto et al. highlighted that following drugs treatment of both relapse episodes, the hyperperfusions in the region became normalized. This represents further evidence that OFC hyperactivity is related to the pathophysiology of OCD. Furthermore, among OCD patients, grey matter density in the right lateral OFC correlated significantly with OCD symptom severity, but not with anxiety or depression (Szeszko et al., 2008).

CONCLUSION

Neuroimaging techniques showed differences between OCD patients and controls individuals in several brain areas. Such differences were also found in the few studies which compared OCD individuals with patients with depressive or anxiety disorders. Moreover, in some studies specific patterns of gray matter volume abnormalities in prefrontal cortex and midbrain in OCD patients were associated with the global severity of the disorder. Indeed, different symptom dimensions of OCD, could be mediated by distinct but partially overlapping neural systems.

Research showed activation in unexpected regions of the brain, such as the temporal and parietal cortices, during symptom provocation tasks. Also, different patterns of brain over- and underactivation have been found in some studies where the OCD patients were required to exert response inhibition or were engaed in speficic cognitive tasks. This pattern of activation, which is commonly seen in fMRI studies of OCD patients, may reflect a compensatory response to a primary neuronal abnormality.

Lastly, psychological interventions, such as CBT, may be able to modify activity in dysfunctional neural circuitries linked to development and/or manteinance of OCD.

References

Adler, C. M., McDonough-Ryan, P., Sax, K. W., Holland, S. K., Arndt, S., & Strakowski, S. M. (2000). fMRI of neuronal activation with symptom provocation in unmedicated patients with obsessive-compulsive disorder. *Journal of Psychiatric Research, 34*(4-5), 317-324.

Alptekin, K., Degirmenci, B., Kivircik, B. B., Durak, H., Yemez, B., Derebek, E., et al. (2001). Tc-99m HMPAO brain perfusion SPECT in drug-free obsessive-compulsive patients without depression. *Psychiatry Research, 107*(1), 51-56.

Andreasen, N. C., Paradiso, S., & O'Leary, D. S. (1998). "Cognitive dysmetria" as an integrative theory of schizophrenia: A dysfunction in cortical-subcortical-cerebellar circuitry? *Schizophrenia Bulletin, 24*(2), 203-218.

Baxter, L. R., Schwartz, J. M., Berman, K. S., Szuba, M. P., Guze, B. H., Mazziotta, J. C., et al. (1992). Caudate glucose metabolite changes with both drug and behavior therapy for obsessive-compulsive disorder. *Archives of General Psychiatry, 49*(9), 681-689.

Baxter, L. R., Schwartz, J. M., Mazziotta, J. C., Phelps, M. D., Pahl, J. J., Guze, B. H., et al. (1988). Cerebral glucose metabolic rates in nondepressed patients with obsessive-compulsive disorder. *American Journal of Psychiatry, 145*(12), 1560-1563.

Braver, T. S., Barch, D. M., Gray, J. R., Molfese, D. L., & Snyder, A. (2001). Anterior cingulate cortex and response conflict: Effects of frequency, inhibition and errors. *Cerebral Cortex, 11*(9), 825-836.

Brody, A. L., Saxena, S., Schwartz, J. M., Stoessel, P. W., Maidment, K. M., Phelps, M. D., et al. (1998). FDG-PET predictors of response to behavioral therapy and pharmacotherapy in obsessive compulsive disorder. *Psychiatry Research, 84*(1), 1-6.

Chamberlain, S. R., Blackwell, A. D., Fineberg, N. A., Robbins, T. W., & Sahakian, B. J. (2005). The neuropsychology of obsessive-compulsive disorder: The importance of failures in cognitive and behavioral inhibition as candidate endophenotypic markers. *Neuroscience and Biobehavioral Reviews, 29*(3), 399-419.

Choi, J. S., Kim, H. S., Yoo, S. Y., Ha, T. H., Chang, J. H., Kim, Y. Y., et al. (2006). Morphometric alterations of anterior superior temporal cortex in obsessive-compulsive disorder. *Depression and Anxiety, 23*(5), 290-296.

Cottraux, J., Gerard, D., Cinotti, L., Froment, J. C., Deiber, M. P., Le Bars, D., et al. (1996). A controlled positron emission tomography study of obsessive and neutral auditory stimulation in obsessive-compulsive disorder with checking rituals. *Psychiatry Research, 60*(2-3), 101-112.

Edmonstone, Y., Austin, M.-P., Prentice, N., Dougall, N., Freeman, C. P., Ebmeier, K. P., et al. (1994). Uptake of 99mTc-exametazime shown by single photon emission computerized tomography in obsessive-compulsive disorder compared with major depression and normal controls. *Acta Psychiatrica Scandinavica, 90*(4), 298-303.

Elliot, R., Dolan, R. J., & Frith, C. D. (2000). Dissociable functions in the medial and lateral orbitofrontal cortex: Evidence from human neuroimaging studies. *Cerebral Cortex, 10*(3), 308-317.

Frankland, P. W., Bontempi, B., Talton, L. E., Kaczmarek, L., & Silva, A. J. (2004). The involvement of the cortex in remote contextual fear memory. *Science, 304*, 881-883.

Gilbert, A. R., Mataix-Cols, D., Almeida, J. R. C., Lawrence, N., Nutche, J., Diwadkar, V., et al. (2008). Brain structure and symptom dimension relationships in obsessive-compulsive disorder: A voxel-based morphometry study. *Journal of Affective Disorders, 109*, 117-126.

Hendler, T., Goshen, E., Tadmor, R., Lustig, M., Zwas, S. T., & Zohar, J. (1999). Evidence for striatal modulation in the presence of fixed cortical injury in obsessive-compulsive disorder (OCD). *European Neuropsychopharmacology, 9*(5), 371-376.

Hoehn-Saric, R., Pearlson, G. D., Harris, G. J., Machlin, S. R., & Camargo, E. E. (1991). Effects of fluoxetine on regional cerebral blood flow in obsessive compulsive patients. *American Journal of Psychiatry, 148*(9), 1243-1245.

Karadag, G., Oguzhanoglu, N. K., Kurt, T., Oguzhanoglu, A., Atesci, F., & Ozdel, O. (2003). Quantitative EEG analysis in obsessive compulsive disorder. *International Journal of Neuroscience, 113*(6), 833-847.

Kumari, V. (2006). Do psychotherapies produce neurobiological effects? *Acta Neuropsychiatrica, 18*(2), 61-70.

Lacerda, A. L. T., Dalgalarrondo, P., Caetano, D., Camargo, E. E., Etchebehere, E. C. S. C., & Soares, J. C. (2003). Elevated thalamic and prefrontal regional cerebral blood flow in obsessive-compulsive disorder: A SPECT study. *Psychiatry Research: Neuroimaging, 123*(2), 125-134.

Lucey, J. V., Costa, D. C., Adshead, G., Deahl, M., Busatto, G., Gacinovic, S., et al. (1997). Brain blood flow in anxiety disorders. OCD, panic disorder with agoraphobia, and posttraumatic stress disorder on 99mTcHMPAO single photon emission tomography (SPECT). *British Journal of Psychiatry, 171*, 346-350.

Lucey, J. V., Costa, D. C., Blanes, T., Busatto, G. F., Pillowsky, L. S., Takei, N., et al. (1995). Regional cerebral blood flow in obsessive-compulsive disorder patients at rest. Differential correlates with obsessive-compulsive and anxious-avoidant dimensions. *British Journal of Psychiatry, 167*(5), 629-634.

Machlin, S. R., Harris, G. J., Pearlson, G. D., Hoehn-Saric, R., Jeffery, P., & Camargo, E. E. (1991). Elevated medial-frontal cerebral blood flow in obsessive-compulsive patients: A SPECT study. *American Journal of Psychiatry, 148*(9), 1240-1242.

Maihofner, C., Sperling, W., Kaltenhauser, M., Bleich, S., de Zwaan, M., Wiltfang, J., et al. (2007). Spontaneous magnetoencephalographic activity in patients with obsessive-compulsive disorder. *Brain Research, 1129*(1), 200-205.

Mataix-Cols, D., Wooderson, S., Lawrence, N. S., Brammer, M. J., Speckens, A., & Phillips, M. L. (2004). Neural correlates of washing, checking, and hoarding symptom dimensions in obsessive-compulsive disorder. *Archives of General Psychiatry, 61*(6), 564-576.

Matsumoto, R., Nakamae, T., Yoshida, T., Kitabayashi, Y., Ushijima, Y., Narumoto, J., et al. (2008). Recurrent hyperperfusion in the right orbitofrontal cortex in obsessive-compulsive disorder. *Progress in Neuropsychopharmacology and Biological Psychiatry, 32* (4), 1082-1084.

McGuire, P., Bench, C. J., Frith, C. D., Marks, I. M., Frackowiak, R. S., & Dolan, R. J. (1994). Functional anatomy of obsessive-compulsive phenomena. *British Journal of Psychiatry, 164*(4), 459-468.

Modell, J. G., Mountz, J. M., Curtis, G. C., & Greden, J. F. (1989). Neurophysiologic dysfunction in basal ganglia/limbic striatal and thalamocortical circuits as a pathogenetic mechanism of obsessive-compulsive disorder. *Journal of Neuropsychiatry and Clinical Neurosciences, 1*(1), 27-36.

Nakao, T., Nakagawa, A., Yoshiura, T., Nakatani, E., Nabeyama, M., Yoshizato, C., et al. (2005a). A functional MRI comparison of patients with obsessive-compulsive disorder and normal controls during a chinese character Stroop task. *Psychiatry Research: Neuroimaging, 139*(2), 101-114.

Nakao, T., Nakagawa, A., Yoshiura, T., Nakatani, E., Nabeyama, M., Yoshizato, C., et al. (2005b). Brain activation of patients with obsessive-compulsive disorder during neuropsychological and symptom provocation tasks before and after symptom improvement: A functional magnetic resonance imaging study. *Biological Psychiatry, 57*(8), 901-910.

Nakatani, E., Nakgawa, A., Ohara, Y., Goto, S., Uozomi, N., Iwakiri, M., et al. (2003). Effects of behavior therapy on regional cerebral blood flow in obsessive-compulsive disorder. *Psychiatry Research: Neuroimaging, 124*(2), 113-120.

Papageorgiou, C. C., & Rabavilas, A. D. (2003). Abnormal P600 in obsessive–compulsive disorder. A comparison with healthy controls. *Psychiatry Research, 119*, 133-143.

Perani, D., Colombo, C., Bressi, S., Bonfanti, A., Grassi, F., Scarone, S., et al. (1995). [18F]FDG PET study in obsessive-compulsive disorder. A clinical/metabolic correlation study after treatment. *British Journal of Psychiatry, 166*(2), 244-250.

Pujol, J., Soriano-Mas, C., Alonso, P., Cardoner, N., Menchon, J. M., Deus, J., et al. (2004). Mapping structural brain alterations in obsessive-compulsive disorder. *Archives of General Psychiatry, 61*(7), 720-730.

Pujol, J., Torres, L., Deus, J., Cardoner, N., Pifarre, J., Capdevila, A., et al. (1999). Functional magnetic resonance imaging in study of frontal lobe activation during word generation in obsessive-compulsive disorder. *Biological Psychiatry, 45*(7), 891-897.

Rauch, S. L., Jenike, M. A., Alpert, N. M., Baer, L., Breiter, H. C., Savage, C. R., et al. (1994). Regional cerebral blood flow measured during symptom provocation in obsessive-compulsive disorder using oxygen 15-labeled carbon dioxide and positron emission tomography. *Archives of General Psychiatry, 51*(1), 62-70.

Rauch, S. L., Shin, L. M., & Wright, C. I. (2003). Neuroimaging studies of amygdala function in anxiety disorders. *Annals of the New York Academy of Sciences, 985*, 389-410.

Rauch, S. L., Whalen, P. J., Curran, T., Shin, L. M., Coffey, B. J., Savage, C. R., et al. (2001). Probing striato-thalamic function in obsessive-compulsive disorder and Tourette syndrome using neuroimaging methods. *Advances in Neurology, 85*, 207-224.

Roffman, J. L., Marci, C. D., Glick, D. M., Dougherty, D. D., & Rauch, S. L. (2005). Neuroimaging and the functional neuroanatomy of psychotherapy. *Psychological Medicine, 35*(10), 1385-1398.

Rosenberg, D. R., Dick, E. L., O'Hearn, K. M., & Sweeney, J. A. (1997). Response-inhibition deficits in obsessive-compulsive disorder: An indicator of dysfunction in frontostriatal circuits. *Journal of Psychiatry and Neuroscience, 22*(1), 29-38.

Rotge, J. Y., Guehl, D., Dilharreguy, B., Cuny, E., Tignol, J., Bioulac, B., et al. (2008). Provocation of obsessive-compulsive symptoms: A quantitative voxel-based meta-analysis of functional neuroimaging studies. *Journal of Psychiatry and Neuroscience, 33*(5), 405-412.

Roth, R. M., Saykin, A. J., Flashman, L. A., Pixley, H. S., West, J. D., & Mamourian, A. C. (2007). Event-related functional magnetic resonance imaging of response inhibition in obsessive-compulsive disorder. *Biological Psychiatry, 63*(8), 901-909.

Rubin, R. T., Ananth, J., Villanueva-Meyer, J., Trajmar, P. G., & Mena, I. (1995). Regional 133xenon cerebral blood flow and cerebral 99mTc-HMPAO uptake in patients with obsessive-compulsive disorder before and during treatment. *Biological Psychiatry, 38*(7), 429-437.

Rubin, R. T., Villanueva-Meyer, J., Ananth, J., Trajmar, P. G., & Mena, I. (1992). Regional xenon 133 cerebral blood flow and cerebral technetium 99m HMPAO uptake in unmedicated patients with obsessive-compulsive disorder and matched normal control subjects. Determination by high-resolution single-photon emission computed tomography. *Archives of General Psychiatry, 49*(9), 695-702.

Saxena, S., & Rauch, S. L. (2000). Functional neuroimaging and the neuroanatomy of obsessive-compulsive disorder. *Psychiatric Clinics of North America, 23*(3), 563-586.

Schmahmann, J. D., & Pandya, D. N. (1997). The cerebrocerebellar system. *International Review of Neurobiology, 41*, 31-60.

Schmidtke, K., Schorb, A., Winkelmann, G., & Hohagen, F. (1998). Cognitive frontal lobe dysfunction in obsessive-compulsive disorder. *Biological Psychiatry, 43*(9), 666-673.

Schwartz, J. M., Stoessel, P. W., Baxter, L. R., Martin, K. M., & Phelps, M. E. (1996). Systematic changes in cerebral glucose metabolic rate after successful behavior modification treatment of obsessive-compulsive disorder. *Archives of General Psychiatry, 53*(2), 109-113.

Shidara, M., & Richmond, B. J. (2002). Anterior cingulate: Single neuronal signals related to degree of reward expectancy. *Science, 296*(5573), 1709-1711.

Simpson, S., & Baldwin, B. (1995). Neuropsychiatry and SPECT of an acute obsessive-compulsive syndrome patient. *British Journal of Psychiatry, 166*(3), 390-392.

Swedo, S. E., Rapoport, J. L., Leonard, H. L., Lenane, M. C., & Cheslow, D. L. (1989). Obsessive–compulsive disorder in children and adolescents. Clinical phenomenology of 70 consecutive cases. *Archives of General Psychiatry, 46*, 335-341.

Szeszko, P. R., Ardenaki, B. A., Ashtari, M., Malhotra, A. K., Robinson, D., Bilder, R. M., et al. (2005). White matter abnormalities in obsessive-compulsive disorder: A diffusion tensor imaging study. *Archives of General Psychiatry, 62*(7), 782-790.

Szeszko, P. R., Christian, C., MacMaster, F., Lencz, T., Mirza, Y., Taormina, S. P., et al. (2008). Gray matter structural alterations in psychotropic drug-naive pediatric obsessive-compulsive disorder: An optimized voxel-based morphometry study. *American Journal of Psychiatry, 165*(10), 1299-1307.

Tot, S., Ozge, A., Comelekoglu, U., Yazici, K., & Bal, N. (2002). Association of QEEG findings with clinical characteristics of OCD: Evidence of left frontotemporal dysfunction. *Canadian Journal of Psychiatry, 47*(6), 538-545.

van den Heuvel, O. A., Veltman, D. J., Groenewegen, H. J., Cath, D. C., van Balkom, A. J., van Hartskamp, J., et al. (2005). Frontal-striatal dysfunction during planning in obsessive-compulsive disorder. *Archives of General Psychiatry, 62*(3), 301-309.

Yucel, M., Harrison, B. J., Wood, S. J., Fornito, A., Wellard, R. M., Pujol, J., et al. (2007). Functional and biochemical alterations of the medial frontal cortex in obsessive-compulsive disorder. *Archives of General Psychiatry, 64*(8), 946-955.

Chapter 4

Possible Brain Areas Affected in OCD: An Overview

Abstract

In this chapter we summarized the results of the last two previous chapters, in terms of possible brain areas affected in OCD. Several brain areas are deemed to be involved in OCD such as OFC, ACC, caudate, and thalamus. To better evaluate the consistency of these findings, the many limitations of neurobiological studies in general and both neuropsychological and neuroimaging studies in particular, were illustrated. It is concluded that cortico-striato-thalamic brain circuit seems heavily involved in production of OCD symptoms.

Introduction

Substantial evidence suggests that the development of a capacity for self-regulation relies on the maturation of frontostriatal circuits. The clinical presentations of Tourette's syndrome, OCD, bulimia, and anorexia suggest the presence of impaired control processes in each of these conditions, and converging lines of evidence suggest that the pathogenesis of each of these disorders involves anatomical and functional disturbances in frontostriatal circuits (Marsh, Maia & Peterson, 2009). Sensory and motor urges, intrusive thoughts, hunger, and concern with body shape and weight are common in both healthy and ill individuals. Although a capacity for self-regulation keeps these urges, thoughts, and drives under control in healthy individuals, anatomical and functional disturbances of frontostriatal systems may release them from inhibitory control to allow expression of the tics in Tourette's syndrome, the obsessions in OCD, the preoccupation with body shape and weight in anorexia, or the binge eating in bulimia.

Also in paediatric OCD patients, Wolley at al. (2008) showed that frontostriatothalamic dysregulation could affect the inhibitory control functions (which is involved on the pathology of this disorder).

The great part of neuroimaging studies indicate abnormalities in OFC, ACC, caudate, and thalamus, structures linked by cortico-striato-thalamic brain circuit which seems heavily involved in production of OCD symptoms (Baxter et al., 1987; Rapaport, 1991; Rotge et al., 2008). This finding has been confirmed by research on pediatric OCD (MacMaster, O'Neill, & Rosenberg, 2008), and it is possible that the potential involvement of cortico-striato-thalamic brain circuit in OCD occurs in different cultures (Lacerda et al., 2003).

4.1. An Overview

In a recent meta-analysis the brain alterations in OCD were evaluated integrating outcomes from 14 MRI case-control studies that included 371 patients and 407 healthy control subjects (Rotge et al., 2009). It is important to clarify that the studies delineating brain regions with voxel-based morphometry (VBM) were systematically excluded from such meta-analysis. The authors found the existence of a reliably smaller volume in both the ACC and OFC, as well as an increase of thalamic volume in OCD patients compared to healthy controls, suggesting that the thalamo-cortical pathway plays a primary role in OCD pathophysiology. Interestingly, unlike most of anxiety disorders, there is little evidence that the amygdala plays an important role in the pathophysiology of OCD (Rauch et al., 2003).

When considering the cortico–striato–thalamo–cortical circuit, the OFC emerged as one of the most important brain region in the mediation of OC symptomatology. It is important to remind that OFC is composed by a medial and a lateral part (Kringelbach & Rolls, 2004). Because of connections with higher neocortical systems (especially DLPFC), the lateral portion of OFC is presumed to play a role in different cognitive processes: monitoring of error recognition and comparison, selection and judgment of environmental stimuli (Krawczyck, 2002; Wallis, 2007). The medial OFC has several connections with limbic-paralimbic system (insula, hypothalamus, cingulate gyrus) instead

(Kringelbach & Rolls, 2004; Wallis, 2007). This specific region is responsible of cognitive representation of positive and negative consequences that can follow a give action (Fellows, 2007; Wallis, 2007).

Patients with orbitofrontal lesions consistently show behavioral changes relating to inappropriate affect, disinhibition and poor decision-making (Eslinger & Damasio, 1985; Bechara et al., 1994; Damasio et al., 1994). Therefore it has been proposed that the function of OFC is: (i) integrating affective information relayed from other limbic areas, (ii) attributing reward value to stimuli or behavioural response outcomes and (iii) suppressing responses which are now inappropriate. Lateral OFC seems likely to be activated when a response previously associated with reward has to be suppressed, indicating it may play an inhibitory role (Elliott et al., 2000).

Orbitofrontal lesions lead also to reward-related learning deficits in tasks such as reversal learning (McEnaney and Butter, 1969; Jones and Mishkin, 1972; Rolls, Hornak, Wade & McGrath, 1994). It is suggested that impairments in reversal learning reflect an inability to detect alterations in reinforcement contingencies, i.e., changes in the motivational value of stimuli, and to then modify behavior accordingly. It has also been argued that the OFC is relevant in inhibiting previously important, but now inappropriate responses, which would also lead to task impairments following a reversal of reinforcement contingency (Chudasama & Robbins, 2003; Schoenbaum, Setlow & Gallagher, 2002).

As we have seen, the OFC is overactive in patients with OCD (Rotge et al., 2008). Therefore, OFC overactivation might led to an overestimation of the risk that negative consequences may occur following a given action (Aouizerate et al., 2004; Rotge et al. 2008; Whiteside, Port, & Abramowitz, 2004) and to the impaired inhibitory processes that may be responsible for the perseverative behaviors observed in OCD (Menzies et al., 2008). OFC overactivation might also contribute to generate obsessive thoughts that lead to repetitive behaviours intended to prevent negative consequences as a way to relieve anxiety (Aouizerate et al., 2004).

However, as a results of the multi-functional properties of OFC it would be premature to assume that all of its functions are compromised in OCD. While there is good evidence that the OFC is involved in the disorder (Friedlander, & Desrocher, 2006; Pujol et al., 2004), some studies have not found such alterations in OCD or only in a subset of patients, especially in those with comorbid depression (Pujol et al., 2004).

Several neuroimaging studies highlighted the involvement of the ACC in the phenomenology of OCD. The ACC is thought to have an action-monitoring function, playing a role in processing competing information (Braver et al., 2001; Posner & DeHaene, 1994). The cingulate hyperactivity could play a role in abnormal conflict detection as part of an overactive action-monitoring system in OCD (Ursu, Stenger, Shear, Jones & Carter, 2003) and conceivably activate an anterior cingulate basal ganglia–thalamocortical circuit without concomitant sensory input or motivation to perform a behavior, thus causing it to be completed compulsively (Rapoport & Wise, 1988).

It is possible to distinguish a "cognitive" and an "affective" part of the ACC (Bush, Luu, & Posner, 2000; Whalen et al., 1998). Both parts have different brain connections. In particular, the cognitive part connects with DLPFC, parietal cortices and with the primary, premotor and supplementary motor areas. The affective part is connected with OFC, amygdala, nucleus accumbens, hypothalamus and hippocampus (Devinsky, Morrell, & Vogt, 1995).

Paus (2001) proposed that the functional overlap of various brain regions with the ACC provides the ACC with the potential to translate intentions to actions. The cognitive portion is located in the dorsal part of ACC and it is involved in monitoring conflict and detecting error. Its overactivity might generate high "error signal", considered to be the core of OCD symptomatology (Rotge et al., 2008). The affective portion is situated in the ventral part and is involved in the assessment of emotional information and the regulation of emotional responses. Because of its connections with the limbic system, the affective part might mediate the clinical expression of anxiety symptoms associated with the obsessional process (Aouizerate et al., 2004, Pitman, 1987).

In many studies, the thalamus resulted associated to the severity of OC symptoms. The thalamus acts as the final subcortical input to frontal cortex, stimulates cortico-frontal output and plays a crucial role in the processing of sensory inputs and almost all interactions between cortical, subcortical and brainstem nuclei. This permits the thalamus to mediate behavior and cognition. Therefore, the thalamus represents an important relay structure that transmits and processes neuronal information from the basal ganglia to cortical areas (McFarland & Haber, 2002); for this reason its involvement in pathophysiology of OCD seems very likely. Besides the important meta-analytic study by Rotge and colleagues (2008), neuropsychological studies have reported deficits in executive function solely or in combination with memory loss following damage to the thalamus.

Further evidences of involvement of the thalamus in the pathophysiology of OCD come from neurotransmitter and surgical domains. The serotonin, probably the most important neurotransmitter involved in OCD pathophysiology, is densely present in the thalamus, behaving as a complex modulator of thalamo-cortical development and activity (Gilbert et al., 2000; Lebrand et al., 1996). Furthermore, partial thalamotomy has been reported as a successful neurosurgical intervention in treating refractory OCD patients (Modell et al., 1989). More studies are needed to explore the exact role of such region in OCD and which thalamic nuclei are specifically involved in the mediation of OCD symptoms (McFarland & Haber, 2002).

The connections between cortex and striatum have been described as "a common substrate for movement and thought" (Nauta, 1989). The striatum, and the caudate nucleus in particular, is involved in processing cortical information for the initiation of behavioral responses and also has an important role in "procedural learning" and the acquisition of new habits and skills that require minimal conscious awareness (Saint-Cyr & Taylor, 1992). The caudate nucleus has several projections to the OFC, the ACC and the thalamus. For this reason, it has been hypothesized to play a substantial role in the cortico-limbic–basal ganglionic–thalamic systems posited to mediate the symptomatic expression of OCD (Saxena et al., 1998). Some researchers reported changes in the right caudate metabolic associated with behaviour therapy and pharmacotherapy treatments (Baxter et al., 1992) and the modifications in caudate function were found in patients who improved with behaviour therapy but not in those who failed to respond to therapy (Schwartz et al., 1996).

The superior temporal gyrus (STG) is a brain area crucially involved in the processing of visuospatial information and mental coordination (Mayer, Dorflinger, Rao & Seidenberg, 2004). STG has rich interconnections to the amygdala and the OF (Choi et al., 2006; Rempel-Clower & Barbas, 2000), which is overactive in OCD. Therefore, activity of the OF may influence STG activation or vice versa.

Also, activation of the DLPFC has been consistently showed during symptom provocation in OCD (Adler et al., 2000; Nakao et al., 2005a). Dorsolateral prefrontal-striatal loop involves projections from the DLPFC and posterior parietal areas to the head of the caudate, then to the mediodorsal and ventral anterior thalamus via the globus pallidus and substantia nigra pars reticulata, and may be involved in spatial attention and working memory processes (Alexander et al., 1986). The DLPFC is involved in planning processes that seem compromised in OCD patients (van den Heuvel et al., 2005). It is important to add that since depression is a frequent comorbidity of OCD (Stein 2002), depressive symptoms may seriously influence the activity of prefrontal cortex (Maihofner et al. 2005; Maihofner et al., 2007).

More recent studies highlighted the existence of additional structural abnormalities in OCD, particularly within the parietal lobe (Nakao et al., 2005b; Rotge et al., 2008; Szeszko et al., 2005; Szeszko et al., 2008; Valente et al., 2005). These results are in agreement with early findings which showed a negative correlation between some OC symptom dimensions and right parietal rCBF (Lucey et al., 1995; McGuire et al., 1994). The parietal lobe is involved in a variety of executive functions such as attention, spatial perception and working memory (Cabeza & Nyberg, 2000; Culham & Kanwisher, 2001) which, as we have seen, are affected functions in OCD.

It has been suggested that parietal regions operate as part of a posterior attention system involved in disengaging spatial attention (Posner & Petersen, 1990), and there is also evidence suggesting that activity in the parietal lobe is related to sustained attention and attentional set shifting (Le et al., 1998; Hampshire & Owen, 2006; Nagahama et al., 1996). Furthermore, the parietal lobe has also been specifically implicated in other executive functions impaired in OCD such as are planning (Williams-Gray, Hampshire, Robbins, Owen & Barker, 2007) and response inhibition (Horn et al., 2003; Lepsien and Pollmann, 2002; Rubia et al., 2001).

Szeszko and colleagues (2005) proposed that parietal lobe white matter microstructure may play a role in mediating obsessions and compulsive behavior, probably through disruption of cortical-cortical and/or cortical-subcortical connectivity with other brain regions implicated in the pathophysiology of OCD. The parietal lobe may be definitely a focus for future exploration of structural abnormalities in OCD (Menzies et al., 2008).

Atmaca et al. (2008) observed smaller hippocampal and amygdalar volumes in patients with refractory OCD compared to healthy subjects. Specifically, the patients with refractory OCD showed a 12% smaller hippocampal volume and a 23% smaller amygdalar volume compared with the healthy subjects. There is not consensus with regard to the involvement of such area in OCD, but these findings suggest that hippocampal and amygdalar structural abnormalities may be associated with the pathophysiology of OCD, above all on refractory condition. Further investigations could be useful.

4.2. Limitations of Neurobiological Studies

Neuropsychological and neuroimaging studies share a number of limitations which explain the inconsistencies of many results and the difficulty in identifying the cognitive and biological substrates of OCD. The primary issue affecting OCD research is the heterogeneity of the syndrome itself. Dividing patients into mutually exclusive subtypes is difficult as patients are rarely mono-symptomatic. Consequently there has been a shift in focus from subtypes to symptom dimensions based on factor-analytic studies (for a review, see McKay et al., 2004) that consistently report four to five dimensions including symmetry/ordering, hoarding, contamination/cleaning, aggressive obsessions/checking, and sexual/religious obsessions. In fact, specific neural substrates underlying different symptom dimensions in OCD have been described (Mataix-Cols et al., 2004) and different symptom dimensions have also been associated with differential treatment response, comorbidities, and pattern of performance on cognitive testing (Leckman, Grice, Boardman & Zhang, 1997; Mataix-Cols et al., 2002). As such, any examination of the neurocognitive profile of OCD should therefore first characterize the predominant symptoms of the syndrome being examined. There may be methodological limitations involved in identifying specific brain areas involved in the etiology and maintenance of OCD. For example, Whiteside, Port and Abramowitz (2004) found, from a meta-analysis of PET and SPECT studies, that differences in functioning were limited to the orbital gyrus and the head of the caudate nucleus among individuals with OCD compared to non-clinical participants. Whether fMRI and other recent scanning methodologies represent more sensitive methodologies is subject to considerable debate, one of which involves the fact that fMRI, as with all brain scanning methodologies, is a surrogate signal methodology. That is, the site(s) involved are correlates based upon signals detected during the scan, and overlook other minor neural signals (i.e., micro-level neural spikes; discussed in Logothetis, 2008).

To complicate the picture, the prominence of OCD symptoms in rheumatic fever, systemic lupus erythematosus and Sydenham's chorea has prompted studies into the possibility of an autoimmune form of OCD (Arnold & Richter, 2001; Asbahr et al., 2005; Hounie et al., 2007; Swedo et al., 1998). To date it is not clear whether and how such form of OCD could be distinguished – in terms both of phenomenology and neurocognitive mechanism - from idiopathic OCD.

The second crucial issue concerns the implicit assumption of this research field according which it would be possible identify a specific cognitive deficit or brain circuit responsible for such complex disorder. However, brain abnormalities in OCD are very likely represented at a system or network level, where abnormalities across several different regions account for multiple impairments in cognition. For instance, a multivariate method was used to identify two anatomical brain systems: a parieto-cingulo-striatal system, and a predominantly fronto-temporal system including OFC and inferior frontal gyri (Menzies et al., 2008). No doubt, that further work employing multivariate methods or involving connectivity analyses analogous to that occurring in the field of schizophrenia research (Schlosser et al., 2003; Honey et al., 2005), would improve the existing models of OCD.

In most studies another source of concern is represented by small sample sizes, lack of control groups, and inadequate statistical models used (e.g., Muller & Roberts, 2005). Meta-analytic reviews have sought to overcome such limitations with interesting results (e. g., Menzies, 2008; Rotge et al., 2009). However, we should wonder whether studies on ten patients or so may really still offer a contribution to this field.

Clinical and demographic variables may also play an important role in the variability of results. For example, in the studies included in meta-analysis by Menzies et al., (2008) there was a wide discrepancy in population age, illness duration, and medication status. The same authors stressed that that illness duration and medications, for instance, may influence the OFC volume in OCD patients.

In addition, the majority of neuropsychological or neuroimaging studies had methodological limitation related to the inclusion of patients with diagnostic comorbidity. This limitation prevents to reach definitive conclusions; for instance, it is difficult to distinguish the relevance of each disorder in observed abnormalities in brain regions and in patterns activations. The clinical disorders may share similar neural substrates or similar circuits and the interaction between different clinical conditions may generate a very peculiar activation reducing the chance to find evidences. Only a small number of studies have attempted to address such issue by directly comparing OCD and other anxiety disorders to determine if markers are indeed specific to OCD (Purcell et al., 1998b; Boldrini et al., 2005).

Lastly, longitudinal studies have also been lacking in regards to the stability of cognitive deficits over the lifespan (see also, Olley, Malhi & Sachdev, 2007). In general, it is impossible to determine a direction of causality between brain structure, cognition and a clinical diagnosis of OCD without longitudinal follow-up studies.

4.3. Specific Limitations of Neuropsychological Studies

As far as neuropsychology studies are concerned, neurocognitive performance may depend on the test administered; indeed, since neuropsychological tests often involve the simultaneous action and interplay of several functions, it is difficult to isolate any single cognitive component. Most of the neuropsychological tests have been constructed to differentiate patients with well-defined cognitive deficits from healthy controls and thus are not very sensitive measures for the detection of neuropsychological dysfunction in patients with primary psychiatric disorders (for a review, see Kueltz et al., 2004). Also, in disorders like OCD, with an early onset and most likely a prolonged developmental trajectory, the formation of compensatory cognitive strategies is probable to occur and this may introduce confounding elements in the results (e.g. van der Wee et al., 2007).

It is also important to note that neuropsychological deficits in OCD may be similar to those found in other clinical disorders and/or exacerbated by a co-occurring depression (e.g., Aycicegi et al., 2003; Moritz et al., 2001; Moritz et al., 2002; Purcell et al., 1998b). To illustrate, several researchers have speculated that WCST deficits (i.e., dysfunctions in set-shifting), which are inferred to be mediated by dysfunctions of the dorsolateral frontal cortex, may be confined to OCD patients exhibiting co-morbid depressive or psychotic symptoms (Cox, 1997; Malloy, 1987). Moritz and colleagues (2001) provided direct evidence that set-shifting performance is disturbed in OCD patients with elevated depression scores. Moreover, dorsolateral prefrontal impairment, which is considered to be a major contributor to set-shifting deficits (Lombardi et al., 1999), has been implicated in the pathogenesis of depression but not OCD (for reviews, see Rogers, Bradshaw, Pantelis, & Phillips, 1998; Saxena et al., 1998)

4.4. Specific Limitations of Neuroimaging Studies

As we have stressed at beginning of this section, a formidable obstacle in elucidating the specific involvement cerebral circuits comes from their complex structure. For example, there are large a series of discrete, parallel, neuroanatomic circuits connecting the PFC, basal ganglia, and thalamus (Alexander, Delong & Strick, 1986). Moreover, many of these frontal-subcortical circuits exist, originate in nearly every part of the cerebral cortex and project through different subcompartments of the basal ganglia and thalamus (Saxena & Rauch, 2000).

Also, the intrinsic mechanisms responsible for functional and volumetric changes are currently unknown. In fact, compensatory changes due to the "true" underlying neurobiological changes or a number of environmental conditions (e.g., drug use - whether illicit or not -, changes in diet, sleeping, weight) may have biological consequences and cause spurious findings. For instance, increased activity of the orbitofrontal cortex, especially its anterior subregion, in functional imaging studies may be the result of compensatory hyperactivity of residual tissues secondary to decreased volume of this region (Choy et al., 2004). Further research is necessary to investigate this issue, especially at the system and cellular levels.

Since OCD may have pediatric onset in as many as 80% of cases, investigation of its neurobiology may be facilitated by studying the illness in childhood, which may minimize the potentially confounding effects of illness duration and treatment intervention. For example, differences in striatal findings may be related to age differences between samples, which are known to have an effect on striatal volume (Toga, Thompson, & Sowell, 2006). Moreover, the studies with psychotropic drug-naive individuals rule out the potential effects of psychotropic medications on the observed findings (Szeszko et al., 2008).

Lastly, a number of specific methodological issues need to be considered when looking at neuroimaging studies. First, neuroimaging techniques provide indices of brain activity by measuring glucose metabolism or cerebral blood flow; however, the relationship between glucose metabolism or cerebral blood flow and neuronal activity remains controversial (e.g., Dougherty, Rauch & Rosenbaum, 2004). Second, differences in scanning parameters and methods as well as different protocols for defining anatomic regions are important sources of variability between studies. Regard the use of different techniques to observe the several brain regions and the different brain activations, the voxel based morphometry (VBM) provides information about particular areas within a structure that are maximally different between groups, whereas ROI approaches reflect volumetric differences across an entire brain structure. The ROI method requires that regions are manually delineated: a subjective and technically laborious process for which operators must be rigorously trained. As a consequence, in most cases, analysis has focused upon one or two regions within a small sample, limiting statistical power and generalizability of results (Menzies et al., 2008). On the other hand, the VBM method of analysis examines differences in grey matter throughout the brain, without the need to pre-specify ROI for investigation.

Third, differences in baseline brain activity, commonly seen in positron emission tomography studies of OCD (Baxter et al., 1987; Nordahl et al., 1989), may have affected some findings. It would be informative in the future to acquire spontaneous fluctuations in the fMRI blood oxygen level-dependent response during a resting condition (Fransson, 2005) and assess their relationship to group differences in task-related activations. Whereas many researchers have taken the tack that fMRI gives a snapshot of the brain (Bandettini, 2007), others have noted the limitations in the methodology as it is currently applied (Logothetis, 2008).

CONCLUSION

Current findings suggest that the thalamo-cortical pathway plays a primary role in OCD pathophysiology. The OFC emerged as one of the most important brain region in the mediation of OC symptomatology. Several neuroimaging studies highlighted also the involvement of the ACC in the phenomenology of OCD. Thalamus and caudate nucleus have been hypothesized to play a substantial role in the cortico-limbic–basal ganglionic–thalamic systems posited to mediate the symptomatic expression of OCD. Actually, thalamus represents an important relay structure that transmits and processes neuronal information from the basal ganglia to cortical areas, whereas caudate nucleus has several projections to the OFC, the ACC and the thalamus. Lastly, more recent studies highlighted the existence of additional structural abnormalities in OCD, particularly within the parietal lobe. The parietal lobe is involved in a variety of executive functions such as attention, spatial perception and working memory, which are affected functions in OCD.

Unlike most of anxiety disorders, there is little evidence that the amygdala plays an important role in the pathophysiology of OCD.

Many limitations of neuropsychological and neuroimaging studies have been underlined. Inadequate methodological design as well as sampling, the lack of inclusion of important clinical (e.g., comorbidity) and demographic variables and the lack of longitudinal studies may play an important role in the variability of results. Also, in disorders like OCD, with an early onset and most likely a prolonged developmental trajectory, the formation of compensatory cognitive strategies is probable to occur and this may introduce confounding elements in the results. It is also important to note that deficits in OCD may be similar to those found in other clinical disorders.

In evaluating the results of research, we need to bear in mind the specific limitations of neuroimaging and neuropsychological techniques; crucially, the search of a specific cognitive deficit or brain circuit responsible for such complex disorder may be too simplicistic in that brain abnormalities are very likely represented at a system or network level.

Anyway, no doubt that the primary issues affecting OCD research deal with the heterogeneity of the syndrome itself and the complex architecture of neuroanatomic circuits connecting the PFC, basal ganglia, and thalamus.

Such complexity along with the various limitations described, may well explain the difficulty in identifying a direction of causality between brain structure, cognition and a clinical diagnosis of OCD.

REFERENCES

Adler, C. M., McDonough-Ryan, P., Sax, K. W., Holland, S. K., Arndt, S., & Strakowski, S. M. (2000). fMRI of neuronal activation with symptom provocation in unmedicated patients with obsessive-compulsive disorder. *Journal of Psychiatric Research, 34*(4-5), 317-324.

Alexander, G. E., DeLong, M. R., & Strick, P. L. (1986). Parallel organization of functionally segregated circuits linking basal ganglia and cortex. *Annual Review of Neuroscience, 9*, 357-381.

Aouizerate, B., Guehl, D., Cuny, E., Rougier, A., Bioulac, B., Tignol, J., et al. (2004). Pathophysiology of obsessive-compulsive disorder: A necessary link between phenomenology, neuropsychology, imagery and physiology. *Progress in Neurobiology, 72*(3), 195-221.

Arnold, P. D., & Richter, M. A. (2001). Is obsessive-compulsive disorder an autoimmune disease? *Canadian Medical Association Journal, 165*(10), 1353-1358.

Asbahr, F. R., Garvey, M. A., Snider, L. A., Zanetta, D. M., Elkis, H., & Swedo, S. E. (2005). Obsessive-compulsive symptom among patients with Sydenham Chorea. *Biological Psychiatry, 57*(9), 1073-1076.

Atmaca, M., Yildirim, H., Ozdemir, H., Ozler, S., Kara, B., Ozler, Z., et al. (2008). Hippocampus and amygdalar volumes in patients with refractory obsessive-compulsive disorder. *Progress in Neuro-Psychopharmacology & Biological Psychiatry, 32*, 1283-1286.

Aycicegi, A., Dinn, W. M., Harris, C. L., & Erkmen, H. (2003). Neuropsychological function in obsessive-compulsive disorder: Effects of comorbid conditions on task performance. *European Psychiatry, 18*(5), 241-248.

Bandettini, P. (2007). Functional MRI today. *International Journal of Psychophysiology, 63*, 138-145.

Baxter, L. R., Phelps, M. D., Mazziotta, J. C., Guze, B. H., Schwartz, J. M., & Selin, C. E. (1987). Local cerebral glucose metabolic rates in obsessive-compulsive disorder: A comparison with rates in unipolar depression and in normal controls. *Archives of General Psychiatry, 44*(3), 211-218.

Baxter, L. R., Schwartz, J. M., Berman, K. S., Szuba, M. P., Guze, B. H., Mazziotta, J. C., et al. (1992). Caudate glucose metabolite changes with both drug and behavior therapy for obsessive-compulsive disorder. *Archives of General Psychiatry, 49*(9), 681-689.

Bechara, A., Damasio, A. R., Damasio, H., & Anderson, S. W. (1994). Insensitivity to future consequences following damage to human prefrontal cortex. *Cognition, 50*(1-3), 7-15.

Boldrini, M., Del Pace, L., Placidi, G. P. A., Keilp, J., Ellis, S. P., Signori, S., et al. (2005). Selective cognitive deficits in obsessive-compulsive disorder compared to panic disorder with agoraphobia. *Acta Psychiatrica Scandinavica, 111*, 150-158.

Braver, T. S., Barch, D. M., Gray, J. R., Molfese, D. L., & Snyder, A. (2001). Anterior cingulate cortex and response conflict: Effects of frequency, inhibition and errors. *Cerebral Cortex, 11*(9), 825-836.

Bush, G., Luu, P., & Posner, M. I. (2000). Cognitive and emotional influences in anterior cingulate cortex. *Trends in Cognitive Sciences, 4*(6), 215-222.

Cabeza, R., & Nyberg, L. (2000). Imaging Cognition II: An empirical review of 275 PET and fMRI studies. *Journal of Neuroscience, 12*, 1-47.

Choi, J. S., Kang, D. H., Kim, J. J., Ha, T. H., Lee, J. M., Youn, T., et al. (2004). Left anterior subregion of orbitofrontal cortex volume reduction and impaired organizational strategies in obsessive-compulsive disorder. *Journal of Psychiatric Research, 38*(2), 193-199.

Choi, J. S., Kim, H. S., Yoo, S. Y., Ha, T. H., Chang, J. H., Kim, Y. Y., et al. (2006). Morphometric alterations of anterior superior temporal cortex in obsessive-compulsive disorder. *Depression and Anxiety, 23*(5), 290-296.

Chudasama, Y., & Robbins, T. W. (2003). Dissociable contributions of the orbitofrontal and infralimbic cortex to pavlovian autoshaping and discrimination learning: Further evidence for the functional heterogeneity of the rodent frontal cortex. *Journal of Neuroscience, 23*(25), 8771-8780.

Cox, C. S. (1997). Neuropsychological abnormalitics in obsessive-compulsive disorder and their assessments. *International Review of Psychiatry, 9*(1), 45-60.

Culham, J. C., & Kanwisher, N. G. (2001). Neuroimaging of cognitive functions in human parietal cortex. *Current Opinion in Neurobiology, 11*(2), 157-163.

Damasio, A. R. (1994). *Descartes' error: Emotion, reason, and the human brain*. New York: Grosset/Putnam.

Devinsky, O., Morrell, M. J., & Vogt, B. A. (1995). Contributions of anterior cingulate cortex to behaviour. *Brain, 118*(1), 279-306.

Dougherty, D. D., Rauch, S. L., & Rosenbaum, J. F. (2004). *Essentials of neuroimaging for clinical practice*. Arlington, VA, US: American Psychiatric Publishing.

Elliot, R., Dolan, R. J., & Frith, C. D. (2000). Dissociable functions in the medial and lateral orbitofrontal cortex: Evidence from human neuroimaging studies. *Cerebral Cortex, 10*(3), 308-317.

Eslinger, P. J., & Damasio, A. R. (1985). Severe disturbance of higher cognition after bilateral frontal lobe ablation: Patient EVR. *Neurology, 35*, 1731-1741.

Fellows, L. K. (2007). Advances in understanding ventromedial prefrontal function: The accountant joins the executive. *Neurology, 68*(13), 991-995.

Fransson, P. (2005). Spontaneous low-frequency BOLD signal fluctuations: An fMRI investigation of the resting-state default mode of brain function hypothesis. *Human Brain Mapping, 26*(1), 15-29.

Friedlander, L., & Desrocher, M. (2006). Neuroimaging studies of obsessive-compulsive disorder in adults and children. *Clinical Psychology Review, 26*, 32-49.

Gilbert, A. R., Moore, G. J., Keshavan, M. S., Paulson, L. A., Narula, V., MacMaster, F. P., et al. (2000). Decrease in thalamic volumes of pediatric patients with obsessive–compulsive disorder who are taking paroxetine. *Archives of General Psychiatry, 57*, 449-456.

Hampshire, A., & Owen, A. M. (2006). Fractionating attentional control using event-related fMRI. *Cerebral Cortex, 16*(12), 1679-1689.

Honey, G. D., Pomarol-Clotet, E., Corlett, P. R., Honey, R. A., McKenna, P. J., Bullmore, E. T., et al. (2005). Functional dysconnectivity in schizophrenia associated with attentional modulation of motor function. *Brain, 128*(pt 11), 2597-2611.

Horn, N. R., Dolan, M., Elliott, R., Deakin, J. F. W., & Woodruff, P. W. R. (2003). Response inhibition and impulsivity: An fMRI study. *Neuropsychologia, 41*(14), 1959-1966.

Hounie, A. G., Pauls, D. L., do Rosario-Campos, M. C., Mercadante, M. T., Diniz, J. B., De Mathis, M. A., et al. (2007). Obsessive-compulsive spectrum disorder and rheumatic fever: A family study. *Biological Psychiatry, 61*(3), 266-272.

Jones, B., & Mishkin, M. (1972). Limbic lesions and the problem of stimulus-reinforcement associations. *Experimental Neurology, 36*(2), 362-377.

Krawczyk, D. C. (2002). Contributions of the prefrontal cortex to the neural basis of human decision making. *Neuroscience and Biobehavioral Reviews, 26*(6), 631-664.

Kringelbach, M. L., & Rolls, E. T. (2004). The functional neuroanatomy of the human orbitofrontal cortex: Evidence from neuroimaging and neuropsychology. *Progress in Neurobiology, 72*(5), 341-372.

Kuelz, A. K., Hohagen, F., & Voderholzer, U. (2004). Neuropsychological performance in obsessive-compulsive disorder: A critical review. *Biological Psychiatry, 65*(3), 185-236.

Lacerda, A. L. T., Dalgalarrondo, P., Caetano, D., Camargo, E. E., Etchebehere, E. C. S. C., & Soares, J. C. (2003). Elevated thalamic and prefrontal regional cerebral blood flow in obsessive-compulsive disorder: A SPECT study. *Psychiatry Research: Neuroimaging, 123*(2), 125-134.

Le, T. H., Pardo, J. V., & Hu, X. (1998). 4 T-fMRI study of nonspatial shifting of selective attention: cerebellar and parictal contributions. *Journal of Neurophysiology, 79*, 1535-1548.

Lebrand, C., Cases, O., Adelbrecht, C., Doye, A., Alvarez, C., El Mestikawy, S., et al. (1996). Transient uptake and storage of serotonin in developing thalamic neurons. *Neuron, 17*, 823-835.

Leckman, J. F., Grice, D. E., Boardman, J., & Zhang, H. (1997). Simptoms of obsessive-compulsive disorder. *American Journal of Psychiatry, 154*(7), 911-917.

Lepsien, J., & Pollmann, S. (2002). Covert reorienting and inhibition of return: An event-related fMRI study. *Journal of Cognitive Neuroscience, 14*(2), 127-144.

Logothetis, N. (2008). What we can and what we cannot do with fMRI. *Nature, 453*, 869-878.

Lombardi, W. J., Andreason, P. J., Sirocco, K. Y., Rio, D. E., Gross, R. E., Umhau, J. C., et al. (1999). Wisconsin Card Sorting Test performance following head injury: Dorsolateral fronto-striatal circuit activity predicts perseveration. *Journal of Clinical and Experimental Neuropsychology, 21*(1), 2-16.

Lucey, J. V., Costa, D. C., Blanes, T., Busatto, G. F., Pillowsky, L. S., Takei, N., et al. (1995). Regional cerebral blood flow in obsessive-compulsive disorder patients at rest. Differential correlates with obsessive-compulsive and anxious-avoidant dimensions. *British Journal of Psychiatry, 167*(5), 629-634.

MacMaster, F. P., O'Neill, J., & Rosenberg, D. R. (2008). Brain imaging in pediatric obsessive-compulsive disorder. *Journal of the American Academy of Child and Adolescent Psychiatry, 47*(11), 1262-1272.

Maihofner, C., Ropohl, A., Reulbach, U., Hiller, M., Elstner, S., Kornhuber, J., et al. (2005). Effects of repetitive transcranial magnetic stimulation in depression: A magnetoencephalographic study. *Neuroreport, 16*(16), 1839-1842.

Maihofner, C., Sperling, W., Kaltenhauser, M., Bleich, S., de Zwaan, M., Wiltfang, J., et al. (2007). Spontaneous magnetoencephalographic activity in patients with obsessive-compulsive disorder. *Brain Research, 1129*(1), 200-205.

Malloy, P. (1987). Frontal lobe dysfunction in obsessive-compulsive disorder. In E. Perecman (Ed.), *The frontal lobes revisited*. New York, NY: The IRBN Press.

Marsh, R., Maia, T. V., & Peterson, B. S. (2009). Functional disturbances within frontostriatal circuits across multiple childhood psychopathologies. *American Journal of Psychiatry, 166*, 664-674.

Mataix-Cols, D., Marks, I. M., Greist, J. H., Kobak, K. A., & Baer, L. (2002). Obsessive-compulsive symptom dimensions as predictors of compliance with and response to behaviour therapy: Results from a controlled trial. *Psychotherapy and Psychosomatics, 71*, 255-262.

Mataix-Cols, D., Wooderson, S., Lawrence, N. S., Brammer, M. J., Speckens, A., & Phillips, M. L. (2004). Neural correlates of washing, checking, and hoarding symptom dimensions in obsessive-compulsive disorder. *Archives of General Psychiatry, 61*(6), 564-576.

Mayer, A. R., Dorflinger, J. M., Rao, S. M., & Seidenberg, M. (2004). Neural networks underlying endogenous and exogenous visual-spatial orienting. *Neuroimage, 23*(2), 534-541.

McEnaney, K. W., & Butter, C. M. (1969). Perseveration of responding and nonresponding in monkeys with orbital frontal ablations. *Journal of Comparative and Physiological Psychology, 68*(4), 558-561.

McFarland, N. R., & Haber, S. N. (2002). Thalamic relay nuclei of the basal ganglia form both reciprocal and nonreciprocal cortical connections, linking multiple frontal cortical areas. *Journal of Neuroscience, 22*(18), 8117-8132.

McGuire, P., Bench, C. J., Frith, C. D., Marks, I. M., Frackowiak, R. S., & Dolan, R. J. (1994). Functional anatomy of obsessive-compulsive phenomena. *British Journal of Psychiatry, 164*(4), 459-468.

McKay, D., Abramowitz, J. S., Calamari, J. E., Kyrios, M., Radomsky, A. S., Sookman, D., et al. (2004). A critical evaluation of obsessive-compulsive disorder subtypes: Symptoms versus mechanisms. *Clinical Psychology Review, 24*, 283-313.

Menzies, L. A., Chamberlain, S. R., Laird, A. R., Thelen, S. M., Sahakian, B. J., & Bullmore, E. T. (2008). Integrating evidence from neuroimaging and neuropsychological studies of obsessive-compulsive disorder: The orbitofronto-striatal model revisited. *Neuroscience and Biobehavioral Reviews, 32*(3), 525-549.

Modell, J. G., Mountz, J. M., Curtis, G. C., & Greden, J. F. (1989). Neurophysiologic dysfunction in basal ganglia/limbic striatal and thalamocortical circuits as a pathogenetic mechanism of obsessive-compulsive disorder. *Journal of Neuropsychiatry and Clinical Neurosciences, 1*(1), 27-36.

Moritz, S., Birkner, C., Kloss, M., Jacobsen, D., Fricke, S., Bothern, A., et al. (2001). Impact of comorbid depressive symptoms on neuropsychological performance in obsessive-compulsive disorder. *Journal of Abnormal Psychology, 110*(4), 653-657.

Moritz, S., Birkner, C., Kloss, M., Jahn, H., Hand, I., Haasen, C., et al. (2002). Executive functioning in obsessive-compulsive disorder, unipolar depression, and schizophrenia. *Archives of Clinical Neuropsychology, 17*(5), 477-483.

Muller, J., & Roberts, J. E. (2005). Memory and attention in obsessive-compulsive disorder: A review. *Journal of Anxiety Disorders, 19*(1), 1-28.

Nagahama, Y., Fukuyama, H., Yamauchi, H., Matsuzaki, S., Konishi, J., Shibasaki, H., et al. (1996). Cerebral activation during performance of a card sorting test. *Brain, 119*, 1667-1675.

Nakao, T., Nakagawa, A., Yoshiura, T., Nakatani, E., Nabeyama, M., Yoshizato, C., et al. (2005a). A functional MRI comparison of patients with obsessive-compulsive disorder and normal controls during a chinese character Stroop task. *Psychiatry Research: Neuroimaging, 139*(2), 101-114.

Nakao, T., Nakagawa, A., Yoshiura, T., Nakatani, E., Nabeyama, M., Yoshizato, C., et al. (2005b). Brain activation of patients with obsessive-compulsive disorder during neuropsychological and symptom provocation tasks before and after symptom improvement: A functional magnetic resonance imaging study. *Biological Psychiatry, 57*(8), 901-910.

Nauta, W. J. H. (1989). Reciprocal links of the corpus striatum with cortex and limbic system: A common substrate for movement and thought? . In J. Muleller (Ed.), *Neurology and Psychiatry: A meeting of minds* (pp. 43-63). New York: Karger.

Nordahl, T. E., Benkelfat, C., Semple, W. E., Gross, M., King, A. C., & Cohen, R. M. (1989). Cerebral glucose metabolic rates in obsessive compulsive disorder. *Neuropsychopharmacology, 2*(1), 23-28.

Olley, A., Malhi, G., & Sachdev, P. (2007). Memory and executive functioning in obsessive-compulsive disorder: A selective review. *Journal of Affective Disorders, 104*(1-3), 15-23.

Paus, T. (2001). Primate anterior cingulate cortex: Where motor control, drive and cognition interface. *Nature Neuroscience, 2*(6), 417-424.

Pitman, R. K. A. (1987). A cybernetic model of obsessive-compulsive psychopathology. *Comprehensive Psychiatry, 28*(4), 334-343.

Posner, M. I., & Dehaene, S. (1994). Attentional networks. *Trends in Neurosciences, 17*(2), 75-79.

Posner, M. I., & Petersen, S. E. (1990). The attention system of the human brain. *Annual Review of Neuroscience, 13*, 25-42.

Pujol, J., Soriano-Mas, C., Alonso, P., Cardoner, N., Menchon, J. M., Deus, J., et al. (2004). Mapping structural brain alterations in obsessive-compulsive disorder. *Archives of General Psychiatry, 61*(7), 720-730.

Purcell, R., Maruff, P., Kyrios, M., & Pantelis, C. (1998b). Neuropsychological deficits in obsessive-compulsive disorder: A comparison with unipolar depression, panic disorder, and normal controls. *Archives of General Psychiatry, 55*(5), 415-423.

Rapoport, J. L. (1991). Recent advances in obsessive-compulsive disorder. *Neuropsychopharmacology, 5*(1), 1-10.

Rapoport, J. L., & Wise, S. P. (1988). Obsessive-compulsive disorder: Evidence for basal ganglia dysfunction. *Psychopharmacology Bulletin, 24*(3), 380-384.

Rauch, S. L., Shin, L. M., & Wright, C. I. (2003). Neuroimaging studies of amygdala function in anxiety disorders. *Annals of the New York Academy of Sciences, 985*, 389-410.

Rempel-Clower, N. L., & Barbas, H. (2000). The laminar pattern of connections between prefrontal and anterior temporal cortices in the Rhesus monkey is related to cortical structure and function. *Cerebral Cortex, 10*(9), 851-865.

Rogers, M. A., Bradshaw, J. L., Pantelis, C., & Phillips, J. G. (1998). Frontostriatal deficits in unipolar major depression. *Brain Research Bulletin, 47*(4), 297-310.

Rolls, E. T., Hornak, J., Wade, D., & McGrath, J. (1994). Emotion-related learning in patients with social and emotional changes associated with frontal lobe damage. *Journal of Neurology, Neurosurgery and Psychiatry, 57*(12), 1518-1524.

Rotge, J. Y., Guehl, D., Dilharreguy, B., Cuny, E., Tignol, J., Bioulac, B., et al. (2008). Provocation of obsessive-compulsive symptoms: A quantitative voxel-based meta-analysis of functional neuroimaging studies. *Journal of Psychiatry and Neuroscience, 33*(5), 405-412.

Rotge, J. Y., Guehl, D., Dilharreguy, B., Tignol, J., Bioulac, B., Allard, M., et al. (2009). Meta-analysis of brain volume changes in obsessive-compulsive disorder. *Biological Psychiatry, 65*(1), 75-83.

Rubia, K., Overmeyer, S., Taylor, E., Brammer, M. J., Williams, S. C. R., Simmons, A., et al. (2001). Mapping motor inhibition: Conjunctive brain activations across different versions of go/no-go and stop tasks. *NeuroImage, 13*, 250-261.

Saint-Cyr, J. A., & Taylor, A. E. (1992). The mobilization of procedural learning: The "key signature" of the basal ganglia. In L. R. Squire & N. Butters (Eds.), *Neuropsychology of memory* (pp. 188-202). New York, NY: Guilford Press.

Saxena, S., & Rauch, S. L. (2000). Functional neuroimaging and the neuroanatomy of obsessive-compulsive disorder. *Psychiatric Clinics of North America, 23*(3), 563-586.

Saxena, S., Brody, A. L., Schwartz, J. M., & Baxter, L. R. (1998). Neuroimaging and frontal-subcortical circuitry in obsessive-compulsive disorder. *British Journal of Psychiatry, 173*(Suppl 35), 26-37.

Schlosser, R., Gesierich, T., Kaufmann, B., Vucurevic, G., Hunsche, S., Gawehn, J., et al. (2003). Altered effective connectivity during working memory performance in schizophrenia: A study with fMRI and structural equation modeling. *Neuroimage, 19*(3), 751-763.

Schoenbaum, G., Setlow, B., & Gallagher, M. (2002). The orbitofrontal cortex: Modeling prefrontal function in rats. In L. Squire & D. Schacter

(Eds.), *The neuropsychology of memory* (pp. 463-477). New York: Guilford Press.

Schwartz, J. M., Stoessel, P. W., Baxter, L. R., Martin, K. M., & Phelps, M. E. (1996). Systematic changes in cerebral glucose metabolic rate after successful behavior modification treatment of obsessive-compulsive disorder. *Archives of General Psychiatry, 53*(2), 109-113.

Stein, D. J. (2002). Obsessive-compulsive disorder. *The Lancet, 360*(9330), 397-405.

Swedo, S. E., Leonard, H. L., Garvey, M. A., Mittleman, B., Allen, A. J., Perlmutter, S., et al. (1998). Pediatric autoimmune neuropsychiatric disorder associated with streptococcal infections: Clinical description of the first 50 cases. *American Journal of Psychiatry, 155*(2), 264-271.

Szeszko, P. R., Ardenaki, B. A., Ashtari, M., Malhotra, A. K., Robinson, D., Bilder, R. M., et al. (2005). White matter abnormalitics in obsessive-compulsive disorder: A diffusion tensor imaging study. *Archives of General Psychiatry, 62*(7), 782-790.

Szeszko, P. R., Christian, C., MacMaster, F., Lencz, T., Mirza, Y., Taormina, S. P., et al. (2008). Gray matter structural alterations in psychotropic drug-naive pediatric obsessive-compulsive disorder: An optimized voxel-based morphometry study. *American Journal of Psychiatry, 165*(10), 1299-1307.

Toga, A. W., Thompson, P. M., & Sowell, E. R. (2006). Mapping brain maturation. *Trends in Neurosciences, 29*(3), 148-159.

Ursu, S., Stenger, V. A., Shear, M. K., Jones, M. R., & Carter, C. S. (2003). Overactive action monitoring in obsessive-compulsive disorder: Evidence from functional magnetic resonance imaging. *Psychological Science, 14*(4), 347-353.

Valente, A. A., Miguel, E. C., Castro, C. C., Amaro, E., Duran, F. L. S., Buchpiguel, C. A., et al. (2005). Regional gray matter abnormalities in obsessive-compulsive disorder: A voxel-based morphometry study. *Biological Psychiatry, 58*(6), 479-487.

van den Heuvel, O. A., Veltman, D. J., Groenewegen, H. J., Cath, D. C., van Balkom, A. J., van Hartskamp, J., et al. (2005). Frontal-striatal dysfunction during planning in obsessive-compulsive disorder. *Archives of General Psychiatry, 62*(3), 301-309.

van der Wee, N. J., Ramsey, N. F., van Megen, H. J. G. M., Denys, D., Westenberg, H. G. M., & Kahn, R. S. (2007). Spatial working memory in obsessive-compulsive disorder improves with clinical response: A functional MRI study. *European Neuropsychopharmacology, 17*(1), 16-23.

Wallis, J. D. (2007). Orbitofrontal cortex and its contribution to decision-making. *Annual Review of Neuroscience, 30*, 31-56.

Whalen, P. J., Bush, G., McNally, R. J., Wilhelm, S., McInerney, S. C., Jenike, M. A., et al. (1998). The emotional counting Stroop paradigm: A functional magnetic resonance imaging probe of the anterior cingulate affective division. *Biological Psychiatry, 44*(12), 1219-1228.

Whiteside, S. P., Port, J. D., & Abramowitz, J. S. (2004). A meta-analysis of functional neuroimaging in obsessive-compulsive disorder. *Psychiatry Research: Neuroimaging, 132*, 69-79.

Williams-Gray, C. H., Hampshire, A., Robbins, T. W., Owen, A. M., & Barker, R. A. (2007). Catechol O-methyltransferase Val158Met genotype influences frontoparietal activity during planning in patients with Parkinson's disease. *Journal of Neuroscience, 27*, 4832-4838.

Woolley, J., Heyman, I., Brammer, M., Frampton, I., McGuire, P. K., & Rubia, K. (2008). Brain activation in paediatric obsessive-compulsive disorder during tasks of inhibitory control. *British Journal of Psychiatry, 192*, 25-31.

Chapter 5

COGNITIVE-BEHAVIORAL PERSPECTIVES

ABSTRACT

Prior to the development of the cognitive perspective for many different psychological conditions, a long tradition of behavior therapy existed that showed positive effects in a wide range of problems.

Since the early development of behavior and cognitive therapy, the two approaches have effectively merged. The early behavioral perspective on OCD emphasized learning theory and conditioning as the basis for the development of the condition. It was the result of learning theory that led to the development of the dominant approach to treatment, exposure with response prevention. However, there are some important limitations in a purely learning theory based perspective on OCD that have lead to the inclusion of cognitive perspectives on the disorder.

In this chapter we described the conceptual roots of cognitive approaches to psychopathology. Then, cognitive-behavioral conceptualization of OCD as well treatment strategies were illustrated. We also went more deeply into the main difficulties that OCD cognitive-behavioral treatment has to encounter. Lastly, "not just right experiences" phenomena as promising novel conceptualization to OCD was illustrated, since it appears that cognitive-behavioral model is not a completely satisfactory model of OCD.

INTRODUCTION

The past twenty-five years have been marked by considerable interest in cognitive behavioral approaches to a wide range of psychopathology. This has, in turn, led to a movement to develop empirically supported treatments, with CBT leading the way (Chambless & Ollendick, 2001). Central to the cognitive behavioral perspective on any disorder is the role of specific distortions of thinking that lead to continued emotional distress and behavioral difficulties. This has its roots in cognitive approaches to managing depression (summarized in Hollon & Beck, 2004). In this instance, the central hypothesized cognitive mechanisms associated with depression were negative views of the self, world and future (dubbed the negative cognitive triad). Contrary to assumptions, the cognitive behavioral perspective has not been based solely on a single perspective on any disorder. Continuing with the depression illustration, at the time the negative cognitive triad was becoming a widespread means of understanding the condition, learned helplessness was also attracting attention as a way of conceptualizing the disorder. In this instance, the primary mechanism that gave rise to depression was the attribution to the self (internal), world, or future negative events, while attributing positive events to others (external), situation specific sources, or to transitory causes (both perspectives are summarized and critiqued in Coyne & Gotlib, 1983).

In addition, at the time the cognitive approach was becoming increasingly accepted, many were providing more fine-grained examinations of prognostic signs that would limit outcome. This comes with treatment maturity, as the investigators are then able to confidently move past promoting the approach and comfortably discuss its limits and means for producing better outcomes by deviating from accepted practice (Foa & Emmelkamp, 1983).

Since the early development of behavior and cognitive therapy, the two approaches have effectively merged. In many instances, behavioral methods are seen as a means of activating specific cognitions that would not be available to the client during the course of discussion in a therapist's office. Accordingly, a number of 'behavioral exercises' have become the norm in therapy, whereby situations that would elicit distressing cognitive biases are deliberately encountered, and clients are in turn instructed in ways to counter these distorted ideas. Other specific methods for challenging distorted cognitions, as well as established behavioral methods such as exposure approaches for anxiety, have been central to treatment packages identified as cognitive behavioral, and these have been empirically validated for the full range of disorders listed in the DSM. Recently, attention has been turned to factors that would limit treatment outcome using the combined cognitive-behavioral approaches to treatment (McKay, Abramowitz, & Taylor, 2010; Otto & Hofmann, 2010; Treat, Bootzin, & Baker, 2007).

5.1. Cognitive-Behavioral Conceptualization

The early behavioral perspective on OCD emphasized learning theory and conditioning as the basis for the development of the condition. It was the result of learning theory that led to the development of the dominant approach to treatment, exposure with response prevention (detailed in March et al., 1997). However, there are some important limitations in a purely learning theory based perspective on OCD that have lead to the inclusion of cognitive perspectives on the disorder. First, most individuals with OCD do not report a learning history with events that would plausibly give rise to symptoms. Second, learning models fail to adequately explain the emergence and persistence of pure obsessions. Third, when untreated, most OCD sufferers report that their symptoms change significantly over time.

As a means of accommodating the aforementioned problems in classic behavioral accounts of OCD, cognitive theorists incorporated appraisal models of the disorder, most notably the account by Salkovskis (1985) whereby it was suggested that individuals with OCD tend to evaluate their thoughts based on an inflated sense of personal responsibility. This sense of personal responsibility has been suggested to account for the full range of obsessional experiences reported by OCD sufferers. For example, if one has an unwanted thought of harming another individual, this thought would be appraised as (a) a result of a personal defect reflecting an underlying desire to actually commit hard and (b) a personal responsibility to repair themselves of this defect, or to avoid any potentially harm producing stimuli lest the sufferer feel increased risk of causing harm to others. This shift to reliance on an appraisal model of OCD marks an important shift from traditional cognitive therapy (i.e., Beck, 1976) whereby spontaneously arising cognitive distortions are challenged as a means of alleviating distress. Treatment trials using that approach have been generally equivocal, in large part because unlike other anxiety problems, OCD sufferers recognize the senselessness of the obsessional concerns.

The original model based on inflated responsibility has been expanded to include appraisals based on thought processes (overimportance and control of thoughts), the relation between thoughts and outcome (thought-action fusion) and exactness of actions (perfectionism)(detailed in Frost & Steketee, 2002). Each of these in some way can lead back functionally to inflated responsibility (Salkovskis, et al., 1999).

There are two cognitive biases that deserve special attention in the case of OCD. First, thought-action fusion (TAF; Shafran, Thordarson, & Rachman, 1996) is a unique cognitive construct that is divided into two major components. First, likelihood TAF is the belief that having a thought increases the probability of the occurrence of the thought. To illustrate, if one thinks of harming another individual, it increases the likelihood that either that person will cause harm, or harm will befall the target individual. The other is moral TAF. This is the scenario whereby having the thought is the moral equivalent to committing the action. An example would be when having a thought of harming someone, moral TAF would suggest that it would be experienced as the equivalent to actually harming the individual. These two forms of TAF can create significant anxiety, and is an impediment to habituation (Rachman, et al., 1996).

The second is perfectionism. Unlike many of the other cognitive biases described here, perfectionism is not specific to OCD, and models of psychopathology that involve perfectionism include a wide range of other problems such as depression, eating disorders, and anxiety in general (Flett & Hewitt, 2002). In this way, perfectionism may be viewed not as a cognitive construct directly tied to symptom expression, but instead a factor that would interfere with wellness as part of a comprehensive treatment package for any individual with OCD. There are some instances where perfectionism leads to compulsive behaviors in general, and may exacerbate symptom expression in primary OCD, such as exactness of ritual completion, or in the case of individuals with scrupulosity. Factor analytic research has suggested that perfectionism is a unique factor in a major measure of obsessive-compulsive beliefs, but that these beliefs, collectively, do not necessarily predict membership in a group with OCD compared with other anxiety disorders or community controls (Taylor, et al. ,2006). Therefore, perfectionism clearly requires attention in treatment for OCD, but in a manner no different than the attention it would warrant for other clinical states where perfectionism increases emotional distress.

5.2. Cognitive-Behavioral Treatment

Cognitive-behavior therapy has emerged as a dominant psychological approach to treating OCD. It is presently considered the first line psychological treatment for the disorder (American Psychiatric Association, 2007). Recent meta-analyses have shown that treatment using CBT, typically a combination of exposure with response prevention and cognitive therapy specifically tailored for OCD, results in large effect sizes (Abramowitz, 1996). However, treatment is not uniformly high across symptom domains (Abramowitz, et al., 2003). For example, individuals with symmetry and ordering symptoms tend to respond very well to exposure with response prevention approaches to treatment, as do individuals with primary contamination fears. It is reasonable to hypothesize that part of this rapid treatment response comes from the readily available corrective feedback that follows from exposure. Alternately, individuals with primary obsessions and hoarding both respond very poorly to exposure based treatment. For obsessions, it again follows that the corrective feedback is either not immediate (such as in those who has fears of inadvertent or deliberate harm) or does not come at all in the course of therapy (such as those with religious obsessions that involve negative outcomes in the afterlife). These problems in stimulus outcome relations often require considerable creativity on the part of the therapist where other indicators may serve as proxies for the kind of feedback sought. The following therapist client dialog is illustrative:

Therapist: I understand you feel certain that if you read books that involve themes of the devil you will increase the chance of eternal damnation.

Client: Yes, that is accurate.

T: Would the devil make his appearance before your death if you were to attract him by reading this kind of material?

C: Maybe. But how would I know?

T: What if we created conditions that would allow for his appearance, but if these are confirmed, you will have a chance to undo it, since you already engage in rituals for this purpose? Say if we notice a change in room temperature, and not your sense of body temperature since that is from anxiety, by using a thermometer. Would that work?

C: I think it would. We could try that.

This dialog allows for certain beliefs to be challenged, and introduces a behavioral experiment that the client may have been unwilling to conduct without the conditions being set in advance. First, the client previously believed the devil's presence was evident by temperature change, but this was actually due to his body temperature changing with anxiety, and not actual room temperature. Second, the ultimate corrective feedback (eternal damnation) is not knowable to us, but proxies can be relied upon in treatment. These are partial solutions, but may allow for means of improving treatment outcome for symptom subtypes that are more difficult to treat.

As for hoarding, the problematic outcome may be due to several important factors. First, it appears that hoarding is associated with considerable different neuropsychological factors than is associated with other symptoms of OCD (see previous chapters). This compounds treatment since the brain areas associated with accommodating the new learning from CBT may not encode and process this material effectively, or may require many more trials. Second, the feared outcomes in hoarding are difficult to access, or are completely absent. Acquiring and saving is not necessarily a protective activity (unlike washing in contamination fear, or checking in certain obsessions). Accordingly, contemporary approaches to treatment for hoarding diverge significantly from that used in other symptoms of OCD (Tolin, Frost, & Steketee, 2007). Third, most clients with hoarding do not see the problem as interfering, and often do not actively seek treatment or are ambivalent about changing. These factors are among the reasons that contemporary treatment for hoarding is based on a separate model of the problem, and has led many researchers to suggest that hoarding is not really part of OCD at all (Pertusa et al., 2008).

Further, there are numerous other complications in the disorder, not characterized by any one dimension that significantly interferes with treatment (Abramowitz, McKay, & Taylor, 2008a, b). For example, scrupulosity, whereby sufferers feel that the symptoms are morally necessary, creates significant problems in implementing cognitive-behavioral approaches. This is most evident in religious obsessions, or in clients for whom their symptoms revolve around religious observance. Here the clinician is presented with a dilemma involving the methods of treatment and potentially running afoul of religious observance. For example, in more pious or orthodox communities, exposure approaches to religious obsessions can be problematic as clinicians may be less familiar with the accepted boundaries of religious observance.

Another factor that can seriously impede treatment is the presence of overvalued ideation. In this instance, individuals feel that the symptom expression is essential, and that if others were aware of the risks taken then the rituals would be the norm, rather than the exception. To illustrate, while many individuals with contamination fear are concerned with contracting illness, some are convinced that the washing is essential in protecting them from serious ailments. Other individuals who do not take the same level of precaution around contaminants, rather than envied for their sense of freedom, are looked down upon as fools for taking such risks, and if they were aware of the risks in the same way the client was, there would be greater caution taken. This sets the occasion for dispute between therapist and client in implementing exposure treatment, since the client will not accept the treatment as credible. In cases such as these, alternative approaches may be necessary. Depending on how limited the client may be in functioning, it may be necessary to engage in other behavioral methods (such as social skills training, McKay & Neziroglu, 1996) motivational interviewing, or opportunistic exposure during occasions where overvalued ideas are momentarily lower (McKay & McKiernan, 2005).

Finally, in addition to the individual differences between sufferers in scrupulosity, overvalued ideation, and presenting symptoms, it has recently been shown that some dimensions are associated with emotional states other than anxiety. For example, it has been shown that contamination obsessions and cleaning compulsions are a result of disgust reactions rather than fear (McKay & Moretz, 2009). While exposure based approaches for disgust may be effective, preliminary data suggest that it may respond more slowly to intervention, at least among individuals with contamination fear (McKay, 2006). In a sense, this has necessitated simply continuing the former approach involving exposure, but doing so for a longer period of time. The research on this approach is in its very early stages, and it may yet be determined that other approaches will work better, or methods of augmenting exposure will arise that will hasten the pace of habituation. The varied, and in some cases limited, response to either CBT or pharmacotherapy has been suggested by some as evidence of the biological substrate of the disorder (Stein et al., 2001). However, as we have showed here, in research relying on neuropsychological and brain imaging methodologies, a consistent pattern of biological factors associated with the disorder has yet to be determined.

Overall, CBT has shown great promise in the treatment of OCD. While there are a number of caveats, treatment has alleviate symptoms for a vast number of sufferers. Given that research is active and vigorous in this area, it is reasonable to expect progress to continue for the various complications that mark the disorder.

5.3. "Not Just Right Experiences" as a Putative Marker of OCD

In an effort to identify other constructs and processes relevant to OCD, some scholars have turned their attention to the phenomenon labeled "not just right experiences" (NJREs). This is defined as "the subjective sense that something isn't just as it should be", an unsettled feeling because something in the individual or in the world around them is not right (Coles, Frost, Heimberg, & Rhéaume, 2003). One reason for interest in this construct is that it well fits clients' descriptions of their OCD symptoms. OCD patients talk about a tormenting sense of dissatisfaction with their current state, profound feelings of imperfection regarding their need for experiences to conform to exact, yet often inexpressible criteria. In addition, clinicians have long observed NJREs among clients with OCD. In 1903 Janet wrote of "an inner sense of imperfection" and described the experience as follows: "they feel that actions that they perform are incompletely achieved or that they do not produce the sought-for satisfaction" (Pitman, 1987_b, p. 226). Other authors have described analogous phenomena in different terms: *sense of incompleteness* (Rasmussen & Eisen, 1992), *feeling of knowing* (Rapoport, 1991), *just right perceptions* (Leckman, Walker, Goodman, Pauls, & Cohen, 1994), *sensory phenomena* (Miguel et al., 2000). In fact, a deficit in the ability to use emotional experience and sensory feedback to guide behavior (an emotional indicator that lets one know when a state has been satisfactorily achieved) seems coherent with the clinical presentation of OCD (see Summerfeldt, 2004, for an excellent introduction to this concept).

NJREs seem also to capture the perfectionistic-like quality of OCD. It has long been suggested that perfectionistic thinking contributes to specific types of obsessions and compulsions, for instance, doubts about whether a task has been completed correctly and checking or washing until it feels ''just right'' (McFall & Wollersheim, 1979). Studies with non-clinical samples have found perfectionistic attitudes such as "concern over mistakes" and "doubts about actions" to be positively correlated with total scores on self report measures of OCD features (e.g., Frost, Marten, Lahart, & Rosenblate, 1990; Rhéaume, Freeston, Dugas, Letarte, & Ladouceur, 1995). Likewise, Julien et al. (2006) found that perfectionism predicted checking and precision in OCD patients. Actually, NJREs-like concepts (sensations of imperfection) have frequently been discussed in empirical work on subgroups of individuals with OCD (Baer, 1994; Calamari, Wiegartz, & Janeck, 1999; see also Tozzi et al. 2004).

Concepts similar to NJREs have been also included in some theoretical models of OCD. The cybernetic model of OCD (Pitman, 1987_a) proposes that the core problem in OCD is a mismatch between the perceptual input and internal reference signals (i.e., expectations). Summerfeldt and colleagues posit the existence of two continuous orthogonal core dimensions—harm avoidance and incompleteness—that cut across overt symptoms and, in combination, may underlie most manifestations of OCD (Summerfeldt, Richter, Antony & Swinson, 1999). The intriguing model by Szechtman and Woody (2004) contends that OCD stems from an inability to generate the normal "feeling of knowing" that would otherwise signal task completion and terminate the expression of a security motivational system.

Additionally, biological models of OCD seem highly compatible with the concept of NJREs. Dysregulated activity in frontostriatal system is proposed to underlie the enhanced response monitoring often observed in patients with OCD (e.g., Brieter et al., 1996; Gehring, Himle, & Nisenson, 2000) and may manifest as persistent "error signals" erroneously prompting the individual to (fruitless) corrective action (Maltby, Tolin, Worhunsky, O'Keefe & Kiehl, 2005; Pitman, 1987_a; Schwartz, 1999; Szechtman & Woody, 2004; Van Veen & Carter, 2002).

Which data do support the role of NJREs in OCD? Leckman et al. (1994) found that a large proportion of 177 individuals with OCD (with or without a comorbid tic disorder) reported the occurrence of just right perceptions at some point in their illness (92%); these experiences were positively related to the severity of OCD features (see also Leckman et al., 1995). In another study, 63% of 40 individuals with OCD with or without Tourette's Disorder endorsed repetitive behaviors preceded by feelings of things not being just right (Miguel et al., 2000). In two studies with large undergraduate samples, Coles et al. (2003) reported that NJREs were a common occurrence and that they were significantly related to OCD features. Further, NJREs were significantly more strongly correlated with OCD symptoms than other domains of psychopathology (e.g., social anxiety, worry, depression). In a study carried out by our group, OCD patients showed more errors of omission than persons without psychopathology in a Go-No Go task. Interestingly, there was a significant correlation between NJREs severity and errors of omission, whereas no significant correlation between OCD severity and Go-No Go performances (errors and reaction times) emerged (Ghisi et al., in preparation).

Experimentally induced NJREs produced distress and urges to change something, but not feared consequences, in undergraduate students (Coles, Heimberg, Frost, & Steketee, 2005). This is consistent with conceptualizations of compulsions aimed at reducing a sensation of something being not just right or feeling incomplete. In the same study, many significant relationships were revealed between NJREs and OCD-related constructs, while none were found with non-OCD-related constructs (Coles et al., 2005).

Lastly, Ghisi, Chiri, Sanavio, Marchetti and Sica (submitted), administered measures of NJREs, OCD symptoms, general distress (i.e., anxiety, and depression), and perfectionism to a large sample of college students and a small sample of OCD and non-OCD patients. A specific association between NJREs severity and OCD symptoms was found in the non-clinical sample: after controlling for anxiety, depression and perfectionism the NJRE-Q-R Severity score remained significantly correlated with OCD symptoms. The NJRE-Q-R Severity scale clearly discriminated OCD patients from patients with other anxiety disorders or depression. Importantly, the NJREs measure differentiated the clinical groups when OCD beliefs were controlled, whereas OCD beliefs did not discriminate among the groups after NJREs severity was controlled.

So, how NJRE could improve OCD conceptualization? First, NJREs could be formally incorporated into OCD psychological models, given its seemingly specific relationship to OC features. Indeed, many clinical descriptions of OCD indicate NJRE-like concepts as an important component of this disorder. For instance, Summerfeldt et al. (1999) remarked that many compulsions seem aimed at reducing distress rather than at avoiding feared consequences; Feinstein, Falloon, Petkova and Liebowitz (2003) found evidence distinguishing washing compulsions that reduce “uncomfortable feelings” of contamination from those that reduce fears of harm. A recent study of Pietrafesa and Coles (2009) found that self-reported levels of incompleteness (i.e., NJREs) and harm avoidance uniquely predicted participants’ ratings of their experiences while performing OCD-relevant behavioral tasks.

In addition, further research can explore whether compulsions aimed at harm avoidance versus producing a just-right sensation are mediated by the same neuroanatomical substrates. If variations are found, they may have important implications for pharmacotherapy and other biological approaches to treatment.

NJREs may play an important role in predicting treatment outcome. Foa and Kozak (1986) proposed that reductions in OCD symptoms are moderated by reductions in estimates of the probability of feared consequences achieved via repeated disconfirmations of the expected outcome. Therefore, when a feared consequence is not clearly articulated, the efficacy of corrective exposures may be compromised (Foa, Abramowitz, Franklin, and Kozak, 1999; Rasmussen & Eisen, 1992). It is possible that patients who did not articulate feared consequences may have been distressed by NJREs. Furthermore, Rasmussen and Eisen (1992) noted that medication-resistant patients often report sensations of incompleteness (in contrast to feared consequences). Standard psychological and pharmacological treatment for OCD may consequently need to be modified in order to achieve better results in presence of high levels of NJRE.

NJREs might also be considered (and investigated) as a putative marker for OCD, a psychological endophenotype, so to speak. In biological research, an endophenotype is an objective measurable trait that decompose top-level phenotypes into into meaningful markers more proximally related to the etiology of a disorder (e.g., Chamberlain et al., 2008). The glucose tolerance test, measurements of serum cholesterol levels, and sphygmomanometer measurements all represent objective and quantifiable methods; the phenomena measured by these methods constitute endophenotypes. The concept of endophenotypes appears relevant to psychology as well, considering that many psychological constructs are too distal from the underlying pathogenesis of mental disorders to provide sufficient explanative power, clinical pictures most likely reflecting the combined influence and interactions of genetic, epigenetic, stochastic, and learning /environment factors. For instance, the construct of Anxiety Sensitivity (AS), conceptualized as the fear of anxiety and anxiety-related sensations (Reiss & McNally, 1985), may be deemed a psychological marker of anxiety disorders in general and panic disorder in particular (e.g., Barlow, 1991; McNally, 1990; Reiss, 1991). Numerous studies indicate that AS is the best predictor of panic responses in both clinical and non-clinical populations (Brown, Smits, Powers, & Telch, 2003; Shipherd, Beck, & Ohtake, 2001; Rapee & Medoro, 1994) and helps identify people at risk for the emergence of panic disorder or panic attacks following stress (Gardenswartz & Craske, 2001; Schmidt, Lerew, & Jackson, 1997). Moreover, AS is resulted a better predictor of response to panic-provocation manipulations than trait anxiety (Eke & McNally, 1996; Rapee &

Medoro, 1994). Lastly, the clinical improvements on panic disorders are mediated by changes in AS (Smits, Powers, Cho, & Telch, 2004). In the same way, as described so far, NJRE may be considered a possible marker for OCD.

Conclusion

In the case of treatment for the majority of clients with OCD, contemporary CBT holds much promise and many clients enjoy significant treatment gains. The great appeal of cognitive therapy for OCD lies in the theoretical potential to avoid conducting exposure with response prevention exercises (as described in the treatment text by Wilhelm & Steketee, 2006). This, however, belies the reality of treatment. In order to fully access the cognitions associated with OCD, one must typically engage in behavioral experiments, as mentioned earlier. This requires direct exposure to stimuli that would produce anxiety in the service of activating dysfunctional cognitions. It is important to note that many clinicians are reluctant to engage in exposure, even among those familiar with the underlying principles and success rate. There are a number of reasons that explain this phenomena, all of which are easily challenged based on the data. For example, many falsely assume that symptom expression will be redirected to other symptoms (via symptom substitution). This holdover from the psychodynamic perspective on psychopathology implies a hydraulic structure of mind, and is also without any supporting data (Tryon, 2008). Another prominent reason expressed that creates hesitation involves the perceived increased litigation risk associated with exposure. While it is true that exposure increases distress on the way to substantive symptom alleviation, there are no documented cases of litigation for exposure therapy (Richard & Gloster, 2007). Finally, some therapists believe that clients need to retain their safety cues, and exposure will remove these safety signals. This runs counter to available data, where the retention of safety signals tends to lead to poorer treatment outcome (McKay, in press).

While the goal of behavioral experiments is not necessarily extinction, these experiments are expressly designed to activate the relevant appraisals and cognitions typically by doing some activity that is contrary to the avoidance engendered by the obsessions (i.e., someone with harming obsessions holds a sharp knife and points it at the therapist). These behavioral experiments then closely resemble exposure, and are in fact the most therapeutic component of cognitive therapy using the appraisal model (Abramowitz, Taylor, & McKay, 2005).

As noted earlier, since the beliefs described in the contemporary cognitive model are not exclusively the domain of OCD, and that some with OCD do not endorse the appraisals considered part of the disorder (Taylor et al., 2006), it appears that this is also not a completely satisfactory model of OCD. The NJRE phenomenon could represent an improvement of current models in that it well fits the clinical observations as well the descriptions of OCD; furthermore it appears reconciliable with biological explanations of this disorder. Future studies will ascertain the relevance of this phenomenon in OCD.

REFERENCES

Abramowitz, J.S. (1996). Variants of exposure and response prevention in the treatment of obsessive-compulsive disorder: A meta-analysis. *Behavior Therapy, 27*, 583-600.

Abramowitz, J. S., Franklin, M. E., Schwartz, S. A., & Furr, J. M. (2003). Symptom presentation and outcome of cognitive-behavioral therapy for obsessive-compulsive disorder. *Journal of Consulting and Clinical Psychology, 71*, 1049-1057.

Abramowitz, J. S., McKay, D., & Taylor, S. (Eds.). (2008_a). *Clinical handbook of obsessive-compulsive disorder and related problems.* Baltimore, MD: Johns Hopkins Press.

Abramowitz, J. S., McKay, D., & Taylor, S. (Eds.). (2008_b). *Obsessive-compulsive disorder: Subtypes and spectrum conditions.* Oxford, UK: Elsevier.

American Psychiatric Association (2007). Practice Guidelines for the treatment of patients with obsessive compulsive disorder. *American Journal of Psychiatry, 164*, Supplement.

Baer, L. (1994). Factor analysis of symptom subtypes of obsessive compulsive disorder and their relation to personality and tic disorders. *Journal of Clinical Psychiatry, 55*(Suppl), 18–23.

Barlow, D. H. (1991). Disorders of emotion. *Psychological Inquiry, 2,* 58-71.

Beck, A.T. (1976). *Cognitive therapy and the emotional disorders.* New York: International University Press.

Brieter, H. C., Rauch, S. L., Kwong, K. K., Baker, J. R., Weisskoff, R. M., Kennedy, D. N., Kendrick, A. D., Davis, T. L., Jiang, A., Cohen, M. S., Stern, C. E., Beliveau, J. W., Baer, L., O'Sullivan, R. L., Savage, C. R., Jenike, M. A., & Rosen, B. R. (1996). Functional magnetic resonance imaging of symptom provocation in obsessive-compulsive disorder. *Archives of General Psychiatry,* 53, 595–606.

Brown, M., Smits, J. A. J., Powers, M. B., & Telch, M. J. (2003). Differential sensitivity of the three ASI factors in predicting panic disorder patients' subjective and behavioural response to hyperventilation challenge. *Journal of Anxiety Disorders,* 17, 583 – 591.

Calamari, J. E., Wiegartz, P. S., & Janeck, A. S. (1999). Obsessive–compulsive disorder subgroups: a symptom clustering approach. *Behaviour Research and Therapy, 37,* 113–125.

Chamberlain,S. R., Menzies, L., Hampshire, A., Suckling, J., Fineberg, N. A., del Campo, N., Aitken, M., Craig, K., Owen, A. M., Bullmore, E. T., Robbins, T. W., & Sahakian, B. J. (2008). Orbitofrontal Dysfunction in Patients with Obsessive-Compulsive Disorder and Their Unaffected Relatives. *Science,* 321, 421-422.

Chambless, D.L., & Ollendick, T.H. (2001). Empirically supported psychological interventions: Controversies and evidence. *Annual Review of Psychology, 52,* 685-716.

Coles, M. E., Frost, R. O., Heimberg, R. G., & Rhéaume, J. (2003). Not just right experiences: Perfectionism, obsessive-compulsive features and general psychopathology. *Behaviour Research and Therapy,* 41, 681–700.

Coles, M. E., Heimberg, R. G., Frost, R. O, & Steketee, G, (2005). Not just right experiences and obsessive–compulsive features: Experimental and self-monitoring perspectives. *Behaviour Research and Therapy,* 43, 153–167.

Coyne, J.C., & Gotlib, I.H. (1983). The role of cognition in depression: A critical appraisal. *Psychological Bulletin, 94,* 472-505.

Eke, M., & McNally, R. (1996). Anxiety sensitivity, suffocation fear, trait anxiety, and breath-holding as predictors of response to carbon dioxide challenge. *Behaviour Research and Therapy, 34,* 603-607.

Feinstein, S. B., Falloon, B. A., Petkova, E., & Leibowitz, T. (2003). Item-by-item factor analysis of the Yale-Brown Obsessive Compuslive Scale Symptom Checklist. *The Journal of Neuropsychiatry and Clinical Neurosciences, 15,* 187-193.

Flett, G.L., & Hewitt, P.L. (2002). *Perfectionism: Theory, research, and treatment.* Washington, D.C.: American Psychological Association.

Foa, E. B., Abramowitz, J. S., Franklin, M. E., & Kozak, M. J. (1999). Feared consequences, fixity of belief, and treatment outcome in patients with obsessive–compulsive disorder. *Behavior Therapy, 30,* 717–724.

Foa, E.B., & Emmelkamp, P.M.G. (1983). *Failures in behavior therapy.* New York: Wiley.

Foa, E. B., & Kozak, M. J. (1986). Emotional processing of fear: Exposure to corrective information. *Psychological Bulletin,* 99, 20–35.

Frost, R. O., Marten, P. A., Lahart, C., & Rosenblate, R. (1990). The dimensions of perfectionism. *Cognitive Therapy and Research, 14,* 449–468.

Gardenswartz, C. A., & Craske, M. E. (2001). Prevention of panic disorder. *Behavior Therapy, 32,* 725-737.

Gehring, W. J., Himle, J., & Nisenson, L. G. (2000). Action-monitoring dysfunction in obsessive-compulsive disorder. *Psychological Science,* 11, 1–6.

Hollon, S.D., & Beck, A.T. (2004). Cognitive and cognitive behavioral therapies. In M.J. Lambert (Ed.), *Bergin and Garfield's Handbook of Psychotherapy and Behavior Change (5th ed.)(pp. 447-492).* New York: Wiley.

Julien, D., O'Connor, K. P., Aardema, F., & Todorov, C. (2006). The specificity of belief domains in obsessive-compulsive symptom subtypes. *Personality and Individual Differences, 41,* 1205-1216.

Leckman, J. F., Grice, D. E., Barr, L. C., de Vries, A. L. C., Martin, C., Cohen, D. J., McDougle, C. J., Goodman, W. K., & Rasmussen, S. A. (1995). Tic-related vs. non-tic-related obsessive compulsive disorder. *Anxiety,* 1, 208–215.

Leckman, J.F., Walker, D.E. Goodman, W.K., Pauls, D.L., & Cohen, D.J. (1994). "Just right" perceptions associated with compulsive behavior in Tourette's syndrome. *American Journal of Psychiatry,* 151, 675– 680.

Maltby, N., Tolin, D. F., Worhunsky, P., O'Keefe, T. & Kiehl, K. A. (2005). Dysfunctional action monitoring hyperactivates frontal–striatal circuits in obsessive–compulsive disorder: an event-related fMRI study. *Neuroimage,* 24, 495-503.

McFall, M. E., & Wollersheim, J. P. (1979). Obsessive-compulsive neurosis: A cognitive-behavioral formulation and approach to treatment. *Cognitive Therapy and Research,* 3, 333–348.

McKay, D. (in press). Safe, but exposed: Inherent conflicts in safety signal conceptualization. *Clinical Psychology: Science and Practice.*

McKay, D., Abramowitz, J.S., & Taylor, S. (2010). *Cognitive behavioral therapy for refractory cases: Turning failure into success.* Washington, D.C.: American Psychological Association.

McKay, D. & McKiernan, K. (2005). Information processing and cognitive behavior therapy for Obsessive-Compulsive Disorder: Comorbidity of delusions, overvalued ideas, and schizophrenia. *Cognitive and Behavioral Practice, 12*, 390-394.

McKay, D. & Neziroglu, F. (1996). Social skills training in a case of obsessive-compulsive disorder with schizotypal personality. *Journal of Behavior Therapy and Experimental Psychiatry, 27*, 189-194.

McNally, R. M. (1990). Psychological approaches to panic disorder: A review. *Psychological Bulletin, 108*, 403-419.

Miguel, E.C., do Rosario-Campos, M.C., da Silva, P.H., do Valle, R., Rauch, S.L., Coffey, B.J., et al. (2000). Sensory phenomena in obsessive-compulsive disorder and Tourette's disorder. *Journal of Clinical Psychiatry,* 61, 150–156.

Otto, M.W., & Hofmann, S.G. (2010). *Avoiding treatment failures in the anxiety disorders.* Boston, MA: Springer.

Pertusa, A., Fullana, M.A., Singh, S., Alonso, P., Menchon, J.M., & Mataix-Cols, D. (2008). Compulsive hoarding: OCD symptom, distinct syndrome, or both? *American Journal of Psychiatry, 165*, 1289-1298.

Pietrafesa, A. S. & Coles, M. E. (2009). Moving beyond an exclusive focus on harm avoidance in obsessive-Compulsive Disorder: Behavioral validation for the separability of harm avoidance and incompleteness. *Behavior Therapy,* 40, 251-259.

Pitman, R.K. (1987_a). A cybernetic model of obsessive-compulsive psychopathology. *Comprehensive Psychiatry,* 28, 334–343.

Pitman, R.K. (1987_b). Pierre Janet on obsessive-compulsive disorder (1903). *Archives of General Psychiatry,* 44, 226–232.

Rachman, S., Shafran, R., Mitchell, D., Trant, J., & Teachman, B. (1996). How to remain neutral: An experimental analysis of neutralization. *Behaviour Research and Therapy, 34*, 889-898.

Rapee, R. M., & Medoro, L. (1994). Fear of physical sensations and trait anxiety as mediators of the response to hyperventilation in non-clinical subjects. *Journal of Abnormal Psychology,* 103, 693 – 699.

Rapoport, J.L. (1991). Basal ganglia dysfunction as a proposed cause of obsessive-compulsive disorder. In B.J. Carroll & J.E. Barrett (Eds.), *Psychopathology and the brain* (pp. 77–95). NewnYork: Raven Press.

Rasmussen, S.A., & Eisen, J.L. (1992). The epidemiology and clinical features of obsessive compulsive disorder. *The Psychiatric Clinics of North America,* 15, 743–758.

Reiss, S. (1991). The expectancy model of fear, anxiety and panic. *Clinical Psychology Review,* 11, 141-153.

Reiss, S., & McNally, R. J. (1985). Expectancy model of fear. In S. Reiss & R. R. Bootzin (Eds.), *Theoretical issues in behavior therapy* (pp. 107-121). San Diego, CA: Academic Press.

Rhéaume, J., Freeston, M. H., Dugas, M. J., Letarte, H., & Ladouceur, R. (1995). Perfectionism, responsibility and obessive–compulsive symptoms. *Behaviour Research and Therapy, 33*, 785–794.

Richard, D. C. S., & Gloster, A. T. (2007). Exposure therapy has a public relations problem: A dearth of litigation amid a wealth of concern. In D. C. S. Richard & D.L. Lauterbach (Eds.), *Handbook of exposure therapies* (pp. 409-429). Amsterdam: Academic Press.

Salvoskis, P. (1985). Obsessional-compulsive problems: A cognitive-behavioural analysis. *Behaviour Research and Therapy, 23*, 571-583.

Schmidt, N. B., Lerew, D. R., & Jackson, R. J. (1997). The role of anxiety sensitivity in the pathogenesis of panic: Prospective evaluation of spontaneous panic attacks during acute stress. *Journal of Abnormal Psychology,* 106, 355 – 364.

Schwartz, J.M. (1999). A role for volition and attention in the generation of new brain circuitry: Toward a neurobiology of mental force. *Journal of Consciousness Studies,* 6, 115–142.

Shafran, R., Thordardson, D.S., & Rachman, S. (1996). Thought-action fusion in obsessive-compulsive disorder. *Journal of Anxiety Disorders, 10*, 379-391.

Shipherd, J. C., Beck, J. G., & Ohtake, P. J. (2001). Relationships between the anxiety sensitivity index, the suffocation fear scale, and responses to CO2 inhalation. *Journal of Anxiety Disorders, 15*, 247-258.

Smits, J. A. J., Powers, M. B., Cho, Y., & Telch, M. J. (2004). Mechanism of change in cognitive-behavioral treatment of panic disorder: Evidence of the fear of fear mediational hypothesis. *Journal of Consulting and Clinical Psychology, 72,* 646-652.

Summerfeldt, L. J. (2004). Understanding and treating incompleteness in obsessive-compulsive disorder. *Journal of Clinical Psychology, 60*, 1155-1168.

Summerfeldt, L. J., Richter, M. A., Antony, M. M., & Swinson, R. P. (1999). Symptom structure in obsessive–compulsive disorder: a confirmatory factor analytic study. *Behaviour Research and Therapy, 37*, 297–311.

Szechtman, H., & Woody, E. (2004). Obsessive–Compulsive Disorder as a Disturbance of Security Motivation. *Psychological Review,* 111, 111-127.

Tozzi, F., Aggen, S. H., Neale, B. M., Anderson, C. B., Mazzeo, S. E., Neale, M. C., et al. (2004). The structure of perfectionism: A twin study. *Behavior Genetics,* 34, 483–494

Treat, T.A., Bootzin, R.R., & Baker, T.B. (2007). *Psychological clinical science: Papers in honor of Richard M. McFall.* New York: Psychology Press.

Tryon, W. W. (2008). Whatever happened to symptom substitution? *Clinical Psychology Review, 28*, 963-968.

Van Veen, V., Carter, C. S. (2002). The timing of action-monitoring processes in the anterior cingulate cortex. *Journal of Cognitive Neuroscience,* 14, 593–602.

Chapter 6

COMPUTATIONAL MODELS AND THEIR APPLICATION TO OCD

ABSTRACT

Neuropsychology and neuroimaging studies of OCD have revealed various anomalies in brain functioning. On the other hand, cognitive models have also contributed to our understanding of OCD mechanisms. However, the possible causality between biological changes and psychopathology remains unclear and the question of how to integrate biological and psychological data in OCD has not been adequately answered. A comprehensive psychobiological integration is unlikely to emerge from any one particular empirical study; rather, this would seem to require a different research approach. We suggest here that neural net modeling (NNM) in particular, and computational modeling in general, may provide an interesting mean for advancing our knowledge of OCD and putting together the otherwise dispersed evidences reported in scientific literature. In this chapter we reviewed the few existing studies which used computational models to shed light about OCD.

INTRODUCTION

Neural Net Modeling (NNM) is one of the developments of a general approach named "connectionism"; it represents a 'dynamic patterns of activity in a multilayered network of nodes or units with weighted positive and negative interconnections' (Harnad, 1990). The strengths of the inter-unit connections are individually modifiable in a way that is analogous to the changes to the synaptic strength in response to activation. Several principle network architectures with distinct properties have been used successfully not only as models of cognitive functions but also as models for brain structures (Hebb, 1949; McClelland, McNaughton & O'Reilly, 2002; McLeod, Plunkett & Rolls, 1998). Connectionist models have been in ascendance since responses to Stroop tests were examined as emanating from a neural network model distinguishing color naming (explicit task demand) from word reading (implicit task response)(Cohen, Dunbar & McClelland, 1990).

The cerebral cortex can be conceived as a "computational surface" using multiple parallel distributed systems to process information (Ojemann, 1994; Thomson & Deuchars, 1994). The cerebral neurons can be viewed as densely interconnected simple devices forming computational units on the basis of the nature and strengths of their connections. From this simple, but highly interconnected structure, the brain works with rule-based information processing, on problems involving association, categorization, generalization, and feature extraction (Aakerlund & Hemmingsen, 1998; Rumelhart & McClelland, 1986). Therefore, NMM can be useful to reproduce the complex functioning of the brain at a system level. On the basis of a weighted sum of signals from other units the basic computational unit forwards a signal. A learning algorithm allows the strengths of the connections ("the weights") to change in response to input examples, and the network acquires knowledge through reorganization of weights. Neural nets have therefore considerable appeal because of their simplicity and relation to biological neural processing. The capacity of the network's processing elements to simultaneously operate throughout its extent on the subject of its computation (i.e., parallel distributed processing), may really mirror the nervous system functioning.

NMM have proved suitable for modeling psychopathology such as schizophrenia, affective disorders and dementia (for a review, see Aakerlund & Hemmingsen, 1998). To illustrate, Cohen and Servan-Schreiber (1992) described a neural network to model dopamine dysfunction and neuropsychological performance in schizophrenia. The first step in their work was construction of a network that simulated performance of normal individuals on a key neuropsychological test (e.g. the Stroop) related to the processing of context. This network was then 'lesioned' by adjusting the gain of a context module, an effect consistent with the modulatory effect of dopamine on the responsivity of cells in prefrontal cortex. Remarkably, the lesioned network simulated performance of schizophrenic patients on the relevant neuropsychological test.

6.1. Modeling OCD through Neural Networks and Computational Models

Raymond and Owbny (1998) tested trough a neural network model for possible etiologic OCD mechanism: basal ganglia dysfunction, thalamic dysfunction, inadequate dopaminergic inhibitory influence on basal ganglia and excessive input from the limbic system. As target symptom of OCD, the level of certainty about the completeness of an activity such as hand washing was chosen. According clinical observations, persons who do not suffer from OCD would likely associate low levels of certainty with incomplete hand washing, and high levels of certainty with completing the activity. High levels of certainty would also be associated with the ability to quit hand washing. Persons with OCD associate even complete actions with low levels of certainty and thus continue to wash their hands although they are clean.

A model was consequently developed to simulate normal behavior. The network would first be required to associate the completion of a task such as hand washing with normal levels of certainty that it was complete. This was done by creating and training a network that associates incomplete actions (as could be determined by a person from perceptual data transmitted from the thalamus) with low levels of certainty that the action was complete. Conversely, the network also associates complete actions with high levels of certainty that the action is complete.

Manipulations of the networks were than introduced for simulating OCD. Manipulations were of two kinds: 1) changes in inputs to the networks to simulate possible changes in the status of these systems each input represents (e.g., changing the limbic system input to the system to simulate high levels of limbic inputs) and 2) structural changes to the networks to simulate neurologic lesions that may be associated with OCD (e.g., removal of computational elements to simulate the loss of basal ganglia neurons). After each of these structural manipulations, the network was presented with the original training input to assess its outputs after the manipulation. A reduction in certainty, defined as smaller outputs, was thought to be analogous to an OCD patient's lack of certainty about the completeness of an activity.

Lastly, therapeutic interventions in OCD were also simulated. The possible effect on the serotonergic system of the use of these medications was simulated by changing the serotonergic input to the system; to model behavior therapy effects (i.e., reduced level of anxiety) limbic input to the network was decreased, both alone and with serotonergic treatment.

Results showed that only the limbic "overdrive" condition resulted in significantly reduced levels of "certainty," akin to an increase in a patient's subjective anxiety and feelings of compulsion. Behavior therapy alone (simulated by changes in limbic input) resulted in a significant increase in certainty. Surprisingly, by decreasing serotonergic input, level of certainty was significantly increased. Authors commented that this finding suggests that SSRIs may work by down regulating serotonergic systems rather than increasing availability of serotonin in brain systems.

Stein and Ludik (2000) attempted to construct a neural network simulating neuropsychological data on impairment of cognitive inhibition in OCD in order to model neurotransmitter dysfunction in this disorder. To this aim, they chose a test of negative priming. In negative priming tasks, subjects are presented with a priming stimulus (e.g. two simultaneously presented figures – one in red, the other in green), and they have to identify the target (the red stimulus) and ignore the distractor (the green stimulus). The previously ignored distractor stimulus is then presented as the next target for selective naming. Typically, such a task results in negative priming (longer reaction times to previously ignored stimuli). Enright and Beech (1990; 1993) found that OCD differs markedly from other anxiety disorders in this task, since they demonstrated reduced negative priming (shorter reaction times to previously ignored stimuli), particularly when the complexity of the task was increased.

A complex version of this experimental paradigm was chosen to provide neuropsychological simulation data for the neural network; in addition, the authors specified how "lesions" to such a model might have reflected neurotransmitter dysfunction. Results showed that "lesions" of the neural network that corresponded to putative dopaminergic and serotonergic dysfunction resulted in reduced semantic negative priming, supporting a view which emphasizes cognitive disinhibition and the failure of impulse control in OCD.

Kubota and Sakai (2002) proposed that the change of refractoriness in the striatal neurons induced by serotonin reuptake inhibitors could have caused the chaotic behavior of the striatum and this change would be essential for the treatment with serotonin reuptake inhibitors. Neural network composed of the chaotic neurons was then constructed to model the striatal cell assembly, which was assumed to store information related to compulsive behavior. Results indicated that there was a threshold value of the intensity of the refractoriness. If the intensity of the refractoriness was less than the threshold, the output was fixed to one of the information stored in the network (corresponding to OCD symptoms); conversely, if the intensity of the refractoriness was more than the threshold, the output of the network travelled chaotically or periodically among the stored information and did not show specific information (corresponding to the improvement of OCD symptoms). Lastly, the increased refractoriness caused decreased network activity (corresponding to the normalization of hyperactivity in the striatum with improvement of OCD).

These results obtained by the simulation were interpreted in the following manner. In the striatum in OCD patients, the refractoriness of each neuron is weak. This causes the fixed output of the striatum, which always innervates the cortical-striatal-thalamic-cortical loop and leads to stereotyped behavior in OCD. Serotonin reuptake inhibitors can increase the refractoriness in the striatal neurons, which receives the serotonergic input from the raphe, through the second messenger system. The increased refractoriness causes chaotic or periodical fluctuation of the output in both each striatal neuron and striatal cell assembly, which leads to the improvement of OCD symptoms. As refractoriness is increased, the activity of the striatum is decreased and finally the hyperactivity of the striatum is normalized. In addition, the authors explained why there exists a subtype of patients for whom the pharmacological treatment is not useful. To improve OCD symptom, the refractoriness in the striatal neurons must be greater than a threshold. But, in the striatum of these patients, the increase of refractoriness induced by serotonin reuptake inhibitors is not enough and it is still less than the threshold.

Recently, Salomoni et al. (2009) conducted a research on 130 subjects with OCD that was aimed at building a model suitable to predict the final outcome of mixed OCD pharmacological and nonpharmacological treatment approaches. They used symptom dimensions, neuropsychological performances and epidemiological characteristics as predictors. After using a traditional logistic regression, they found that the only predictors of final outcome are hoarding symptoms, repeating rituals and counting compulsions. Moreover they implemented Supervised Artificial Neural Networks, specifically they chose to use for the analysis multilayer perceptrons (MLPs) with 3 neuron layers. Using all the variables considered in the models, MLPs showed highly better predictive performance as compared with the traditional logistic regression models (93.3% vs 61.5% respectively of correct classification of cases)

6.2. Future Directions for Neural Network and Computational Modeling in OCD

The research involving NMM approaches have primarily focused on biological models of OCD. However, to fully appreciate the role of cognitive processes in OCD, one has to examine the primary cognitive processes that underlie the condition. Along these lines, there are several primary areas worth pursuing. First, the neuropsychological test data suggests that memory and executive functioning interact to create problems in organization. Second, memory confidence may play a strong role in doubting. This has been demonstrated in many experiments where doubting can be induced even among non-clinical participants if it involves realistic stimuli (Coles, Radomsky, & Horng, 2006). Third, many dysfunctional beliefs hypothesized to form the basis of the CBT model has been found in subsets of individuals with OCD (i.e., Haslam et al., 2005). And finally, memory change has been identified as an important mechanism in determining successful treatment outcome, and has been used in other studies using NMM (Tryon & McKay, in press).

A critical shift is required in order to pursue computational modeling for OCD. First, efforts to model OCD fully may be untenable in light of the heterogeneity of the condition. It has been noted earlier that OCD is comprised of subtypes (i.e., McKay et al., 2004). While these subtypes have been identified in factor, cluster, and taxometric analyses, they are limited by the definitions of the symptoms and the degree one assumes symptom domains are rightly part of the disorder. This may be subject to change. For example, as the planning process continues for the revision to the DSM, one subtype, hoarding, may be excluded from the diagnosis (Petusa et al., 2008). Second, it has been noted that, to date, no single theory has adequately described OCD (Taylor, McKay, & Abramowitz, 2005). This is partly due to the heterogeneity of the condition, but also because most existing models rely on a deficit model. However, overactivity in specific cognitive functions could be as problematic as deficits in conferring compulsive behavior. For example, recent research suggests that rumination, or an excessive focus on prior events, leads to increased depressed affect (Miranda & Nolen-Hoeksema, 2007).

An approach relying on computational modeling will therefore allow for a greater focus on mechanisms underlying the fundamental psychological processes of obsessive-compulsive phenomena (i.e., doubting, intrusive unwanted thoughts, compulsive behaviors) without the constraints of arbitrarily specified criteria. Given that there is as yet no unified model of OCD, no consensus on neuropsychological deficits, and as yet underdetermined biological processes, a return to basic conceptualization appears warranted. Recent additional approaches beyond NMM hold promise for developing a better understanding of the basic mechanisms underlying obsessive-compulsive symptoms. One such approach, multinomial processing tree models, has been used in other domains to determine the decision making approach adopted for a given deficit or excess that would characterize a clinical condition (Batchelder & Riefer, 2007). This approach is dependent on a Baysian prior probability methodology, and could be useful in describing doubting and in some instances the special rules that individuals with obsessive-compulsive problems experience (i.e., completion after a specified number of repetitions of an act).

CONCLUSION

For more advances in pathophysiology of OCD, it is essential to integrate various observable data. This integration study would require a new viewpoint such as a concept of the brain as a distributed processing system composed of polysynaptic circuits of neurons as information transmission devices, in which OCD can be considered to be dysfunction of information processing.

The connectionist literature has shown that highly interconnected recurrent networks are an excellent architecture for associative memories, perceptual operations and the solution of optimization problems. The ability to respond to graded inputs allows many individual factors to be appropriately weighted, and the availability of many loops of interconnection facilitates recursive readjustments of multiple factors.

It is important to stress, however, that neuron reality is very distant from neural network simulations and that methods used in neural networks to simulate learning have not been proven in real neural systems. Neural networks are simplifications of neural systems that are far more complex. The artificial elements used in computational networks do not always accurately portray all the properties of the neural elements they purport to simulate. Moreover, even the most complex network can model only a small fraction of relevant neural elements and their connections.

Also, many network models explored the effect of certain inputs on the system (e.g., serotonergic) as though its effects were immediate: future models might also consider time-dependent down regulation of various receptor subtypes to address this issue (Raymond & Ownby, 1998).

Whereas further research is required to develop the more refined neuron model and neural network architecture, there is hope that artificial neural network offers a possible way to test more accurately complex models of mental disorders.

References

Aakerlund, L., & Hemmingsen, R. (1998). Neural networks as models of psychopathology. *Biological Psychiatry, 43*, 471-482.

Batchelder, W. H., & Riefer, D. M. (2007). Using multinomial processing tree models of measure cognitive deficits in clinical populations. In R. W. J. Neufeld (Ed.), *Advances in clinical cognitive science* (pp. 19-50). Washington, D. C.: American Psychological Association Press.

Cohen, J. D., Dunbar, K., & McClelland, J. L. (1990). On the control of automatic processes: A parallel distributed processing account of the Stroop effect. *Psychological Review, 97*, 332-361.

Cohen, J. D., & Sevan-Schreiber, D. (1992). Context, cortex, and dopamine. A connectionist approach to behavior and biology in schizophrenia. *Psychological Review, 99*(1), 45-77.

Coles, M. E., Radomsky, A. S., & Horng, B. (2006). Exploring the boundaries of memory distrust from repeated checking: Increasing external validity and examining thresholds. *Behaviour Research and Therapy, 44*, 995-1006.

Enright, S. J., & Beech, A. R. (1990). Obsessional states: anxiety disorders or schizotypes? An information processing and personality assessment. *Psychological Medicine, 20*, 621-627.

Enright, S. J., & Beech, A. R. (1993). Reduced cognitive inhibition in obsessive-compulsive disorder. *British Journal of Clinical Psychology, 32*, 67-74.

Harnad, S. (1990). The symbol grounding problem. *Physica D, 42*, 335-346.

Haslam, N., Williams, B. A., Kyrios, M., McKay, D., & Taylor, S. (2005). Subtyping Obsessive-Compulsive Disorder: A taxometric analysis. *Behavior Therapy, 36*, 381-391.

Hebb, D. O. (1949). *The organization of behavior: A neuropsychological theory*. New York: Wiley.

Kubota, S., & Sakai, K. (2002). Relationship between obsessive-compulsive disorder and chaos. *Medical Hypothesis, 59*(1), 16-23.

McClelland, J. L., McNaughton, B. L., & O'Reilly, R. C. (2002). Why there are complementary learning systems in the hippocampus and neocortex: Insights from the success and failures of connectionist models of learning and memory. In T. A. Polk & C. M. Seifert (Eds.), *Cognitive modeling* (pp. 499-534). Cambridge, MA: MIT Press.

McKay, D., Abramowitz, J. S., Calamari, J. E., Kyrios, M., Radomsky, A. S., Sookman, D., et al. (2004). A critical evaluation of obsessive-compulsive disorder subtypes: Symptoms versus mechanisms. *Clinical Psychology Review, 24*, 283-313.

McLeod, P., Plunkett, K., & Rolls, E. T. (1998). *Introduction to connectionist modelling of cognitive processes*. Oxford: Oxford University Press.

Miranda, R., & Nolen-Hoeksema, S. (2007). Brooding and reflection: Rumination predicts suicidal ideation at 1-year follow-up in a community sample. *Behaviour Research and Therapy, 45*, 3088-3095.

Ojemann, G. (1994). Intraoperative investigations of the neurobiology of language. *Discussions in Neuroscience, 10*, 51-57.

Petusa, A., Fullana, M. A., Singh, S., Alonso, P., Menchon, J. M., & Mataix-Cols, D. (2008). Compulsive hoarding: OCD symptom, distinct clinical syndrome, or both? *American Journal of Psychiatry, 165*, 1289-1298.

Raymond, L., & Ownby, M. D. (1998). Computational model of obsessive-compulsive disorder: Examination of etiologic hypothesis and treatment strategies. *Depression and Anxiety, 8*, 91-103.

Rumelhart, D., & McClelland, J. L. (1986). *Parallel distributed processing: Explorations in the microstructure of cognition* (Vol. 1). Cambridge, MA: MIT Press.

Salomoni, G., Grassi, M., Mosini, P., Riva, P., Cavedini, P., & Bellodi, L. (2009). Artificial neural networks model for the prediction of obsessive-compulsive disorder treatment response. *Journal of Clinical Psychopharmacology, 29*(4), 343-349.

Stein, D. J., & Ludik, J. (2000). A neural network of obsessive-compulsive disorder: Modelling cognitive disinhibition and neurotransmitter dysfunction. *Medical Hypothesis, 55*(2), 168-176.

Taylor, S., McKay, D., & Abramowitz, J. S. (2005). Is obsessive-compulsive disorder a disturbance of security motivation? Comment on Szectman and Woody (2004). *Psychological Review, 112*, 650-656.

Thomson, A. M., & Deuchars, J. (1994). Temporal and spatial properties of local circuits in neocortex. *Trends in Neurosciences, 17*, 119-126.

Tryon, W. W., & McKay, D. (in press). Memory modification as an outcome variable in anxiety disorder treatment. *Journal of Anxiety Disorders*.

GENERAL CONCLUSION

OCD is a very severe disorder which is not still fully understood.

Biological models of OCD have strongly suggested an underlying brain dysfunction, centred primarily in the orbital frontal cortex and basal ganglia. As a consequence, many studies have been conducted to discover possible neurobiological deficits associated with OCD.

On the other hand, psychological models have focused on cognitive appraisals of thoughts. This model posits that obsessions arise from the misinterpretation of normal intrusive thoughts (e.g., misinterpreting unwanted harm-related thoughts as a sign that one is going to act on them). This leads the person to perform compulsions in order to neutralize the thoughts (i.e., checking to ensure that a harm-related thought did not lead to harm befalling someone). Other more complex psychological models hypothesize that a deficit in the ability to use emotional experience and sensory feedback to guide behavior (an emotional indicator that lets one know when a state has been satisfactorily achieved) may explain the clinical picture typical of OCD.

Unfortunately, both biological and psychological models describing OCD do not fully account for the diverse symptom presentation of the disorder. Furthermore, the existing therapeutic approach are not always sufficient for alleviating patients' discomfort.

The book, after a thorough presentation of OCD phenomena, reviewed recent research examining neurobiological functioning in OCD, including neuropsychological test data and functional neuroimaging studies. In addition, a summary of recent findings on the dominant psychological models was presented. For each of these models, specific limitations in depicting the full scope of OCD were highlighted. Research on computational models of obsessive-compulsive symptoms (i.e., neural network, multinomial processing tree account) was also took in consideration.

With this book we hope to offer a general view of the state-of-the art of the most recent psychological and neurobiological research on OCD and to suggest how to go further in order to improve our comprehension of this debilitating disorder.

INDEX

A

D

E

F

G

H

I

N

Q

R

S

T

U

V

W

X